RESTORATIVE YOGA FOR BETTER SLEEP

Relaxing Poses for Deep, Restorative Rest

Helenna Lemann

Copyright © 2024 by Helenna Lemann.

All rights reserved. No part of this book may be used or reproduced in any form whatsoever without written permission except in the case of brief quotations in critical articles or reviews.

Printed in the United States of America.

For more information, or to book an event, contact :
(Email & Website)

Book design by (Helenna Lemann)
Cover design by Helenna Lemann

Introduction

Welcome to the sanctuary of serenity, where restless nights give way to blissful dreams and rejuvenation awaits at every breath. In the pages that follow, you are about to embark on a journey unlike any other—a journey into the sacred art of restorative yoga, where the secrets to deep, restorative rest lie waiting to be unveiled.

Are you tired of tossing and turning, wrestling with the relentless grip of insomnia? Do you yearn for the sweet embrace of sleep, yet find yourself perpetually lost in the maze of restlessness? Fear not, dear reader, for you hold in your hands the key to unlock serenity and banish insomnia once and for all.

Within these pages, you will discover a treasure trove of expertly crafted poses, each one designed to soothe your soul, quiet your mind, and gently coax your body into a state of profound relaxation. From gentle stretches to nurturing breathwork, each pose serves as a beacon of hope, guiding you on your quest for blissful nights and revitalized days.

But this journey is not just about finding solace in the darkness of night—it's about reclaiming your birthright to sleep like royalty, to awaken each morning feeling refreshed, rejuvenated, and ready to embrace the day ahead. It's about transforming your sleepless nights into rejuvenating journeys, filled with moments of tranquility, serenity, and profound inner peace.

So, dear reader, I invite you to step into the realm of restorative yoga and unlock the secrets to blissful nights and boundless vitality. Let the journey begin, and may each pose, each breath, and each moment of stillness bring you one step closer to the restorative rest you deserve. Your path to serenity awaits—dive in, and let the transformation begin.

Chapter 1: The Power of Restorative Yoga for a Good Night's Sleep

Restorative yoga is a gentle form of yoga that focuses on relaxation and stress relief. It involves using props such as blankets, bolsters, and blocks to support the body in various poses that are held for an extended period of time.

This type of yoga is particularly beneficial for those who struggle with insomnia or have difficulty fallingasleep.

Restorative yoga is known for its ability to activate the parasympathetic nervous system, which is responsible for the body's "rest and digest" response. This helps to counteract the effects of the sympathetic nervous system, which is responsible for the body's "fight or flight" response.

By activating the parasympathetic nervous system, restorative yoga can help to reduce stress, calm the mind, and promote relaxation.

One of the key benefits of restorative yoga is its ability to promote deep relaxation. By holding poses for an extended period of time, the body is able to release tension and stress, allowing for a deep sense of relaxation totake hold. This can be particularly beneficial for those who struggle with racing thoughts or anxiety, as restorative yoga can help to quiet the mind and promote a sense of calm.

In addition to promoting relaxation, restorative yoga can also help to improve circulation and digestion. By using props to support the body in various poses, restorative yoga can help to release tension in the muscles and improve blood flow throughout the body.

This can help to promote better circulation, which can in turn improve digestion and help to reduce feelings of bloating or discomfort.

One of the key benefits of restorative yoga for a good night's sleep is its ability to help regulate the body's natural sleep-wake cycle.

By promoting relaxation and reducing stress, restorative yoga can help to prepare the body for sleep and promote a deeper, more restful night's sleep. This can be particularly beneficial for those who struggle with insomnia or have difficulty falling asleep.

In addition to its physical benefits, restorative yoga can also help to promote mental and emotional well-being. By promoting relaxation and reducing stress, restorative yoga can help to improve mood, reduce feelings of anxiety and depression, and promote a sense of overall well-being. This can be particularly beneficial for those who struggle with mental health issues or have difficulty managing stress.

To incorporate restorative yoga into your bedtime routine, consider setting aside 10-15 minutes before bed to practice a few restorative poses.

Some restorative poses that are particularly beneficial for promoting sleep include supported child's pose, legs up the wall pose, and reclining bound angle pose. By practicing these poses before bed, you can help to prepare your body and mind for sleep and promote a deeper, more restful night's sleep.

Overall, restorative yoga can be a powerful tool for promoting a good night's sleep. By promoting relaxation, reducing stress, and improving circulation, restorative yoga can help to prepare the body for sleep and promote a deeper, more restful night's sleep.

If you struggle with insomnia or have difficulty falling asleep, consider incorporating restorative yoga into your bedtime routine to help promote a better night's sleep.

Unwind and Unplug: Restorative Yoga Poses for Better Sleep

In today's fast-paced world, it can be challenging to find time to relax and unwind. We are constantly bombarded with distractions and responsibilities, making it difficult to switch off and get a good night's sleep. However, restorative yoga poses can help you to relax, unwind, and prepare your body for a restful night's sleep.

Restorative yoga is a gentle and relaxing form of yoga that focuses on deep relaxation and rejuvenation. It involves holding poses for an extended period of time, allowing the body to release tension and stress. By practicing restorative yoga before bed, you can calm your mind, relax your body, and prepare yourself for arestful night's sleep.

Here are some restorative yoga poses that can help you to unwind and unplug before bed:

1. Child's Pose (Balasana)
   Child's pose is a gentle and calming pose that can help to release tension in the back, shoulders, and neck. To practice child's pose, kneel on the floor with your big toes together and your knees apart. Sit back on your heelsand extend your arms forward, resting your forehead on the mat. Take deep breaths and relax into the pose, allowing your body to release tension

and stress.

2. Legs-Up-the-Wall Pose (Viparita Karani)
Legs-up-the-wall pose is a restorative pose that can help to calm the nervous system and promote relaxation. To practice this pose, lie on your back with your legs extended up the wall. You can place a bolster or pillow under your hips for added support. Close your eyes and focus on your breath, allowing your body to relax and unwind.

3. Supported Bridge Pose (Setu Bandhasana)
Supported bridge pose is a gentle backbend that can help to release tension in the spine and chest. To practice this pose, lie on your back with your knees bent and feet hip-width apart. Place a block or bolster under your sacrum and lift your hips towards the ceiling. Relax into the pose, allowing your body to release tension and stress.

4. Reclining Bound Angle Pose (Supta Baddha Konasana)
Reclining bound angle pose is a restorative pose that can help to open the hips and release tension in the groin and inner thighs. To practice this pose, lie on your back with the soles of your feet together and knees apart. Place a bolster or pillow under your knees for added support. Close your eyes and relax into the pose, allowing your body to unwind and prepare for sleep.

5. Corpse Pose (Savasana)
Corpse pose is a classic relaxation pose that can help to calm

the mind and promote deep relaxation. To practicethis pose, lie on your back with your arms by your sides and palms facing up. Close your eyes and focus on yourbreath, allowing your body to relax and release tension. Stay in the pose for at least 5-10 minutes, allowing yourself to fully unwind and unplug before bed.

In addition to practicing restorative yoga poses, there are some other tips that can help you to unwind and unplugbefore bed:

1. Create a bedtime routine: Establishing a bedtime routine can help to signal to your body that it is time to relax and unwind. Try to go to bed at the same time each night and engage in calming activities before bed, such as

reading a book or taking a warm bath.

2. Limit screen time: The blue light emitted from screens can interfere with your body's natural sleep-wake cycle, making it difficult to fall asleep. Try to limit screen time before bed and avoid using electronic devices atleast an hour before bedtime.

3. Practice mindfulness: Mindfulness practices, such as meditation or deep breathing exercises, can help to calm the mind and promote relaxation. Take a few minutes each day to practice mindfulness, allowing yourself to unwind and unplug from the stresses of the day.

4. Create a calming sleep environment: Make sure that your bedroom is a calm and relaxing space that is conducive to

sleep. Keep the room dark, cool, and quiet, and invest in a comfortable mattress and pillows to ensure a restful night's sleep.

By incorporating restorative yoga poses and these tips into your bedtime routine, you can unwind and unplug before bed, allowing yourself to relax and prepare for a restful night's sleep. So, take some time for yourself each night to practice restorative yoga and create a peaceful bedtime routine that will help you to unwind andunplug from the stresses of the day.

Finding Peace and Relaxation Through

In today's fast-paced world, it can be challenging to find moments of peace and relaxation amidst the chaos of daily life. However, one practice that has been gaining popularity in recent years for its ability to promote relaxation and stress relief is restorative yoga.

Restorative yoga is a gentle form of yoga that focuses on relaxation and rejuvenation, using props such as blankets, bolsters, and blocks to support the body in gentle, restful poses.

Restorative yoga is particularly beneficial for those who lead busy, stressful lives, as it provides an opportunity to slow down, tune into the body, and quiet the mind. By practicing restorative yoga regularly, individuals can experience a sense of calm and inner peace that can have a profound impact on their overall well-being.

One of the key benefits of restorative yoga is its ability to activate the body's relaxation response. When we are stressed, our bodies go into "fight or flight" mode, releasing stress hormones such as cortisol and adrenaline.

This can have a number of negative effects on the body, including increased heart rate, elevated blood pressure, and impaired digestion.

Restorative yoga helps to counteract these effects by activating the body's relaxation response, which triggers the release of calming hormones such as oxytocin and endorphins. This can help to lower blood pressure, reduce heart rate, and promote a sense of well-being and relaxation.

In addition to its physical benefits, restorative yoga also offers a number of mental and emotional benefits. By focusing on the breath and the sensations in the body, restorative yoga can help to quiet the mind and promote mindfulness.

This can be particularly beneficial for those who struggle with anxiety or racing thoughts, as it provides a gentle and supportive space to practice being present in the moment. Restorative yoga can also help to promote self-awareness and self-compassion, as individuals learn to listen to their bodies and honor their own needs and limitations.

One of the key principles of restorative yoga is the use of props to support the body in gentle, restful poses. Props such as blankets, bolsters, and blocks are used to help the body relax deeply into each pose, allowing for a greater release of tension and a deeper sense of relaxation.

By using props to support the body, individuals can experience the benefits of the poses without straining or overexerting themselves, making restorative yoga accessible to people of all ages and fitness levels.

Some common restorative yoga poses include supported child's pose, reclining bound angle pose, and legs up the wall pose. These poses are designed to gently stretch and release tension in the body, while also promoting relaxation and stress relief. By practicing these poses regularly, individuals can experience a greater sense of peace and well-being in their daily lives.

In addition to its physical and mental benefits, restorative yoga can also have a profound impact on the nervous system. By activating the body's relaxation response, restorative yoga can help to calm the nervous system and reduce the effects of chronic stress.

This can have a number of positive effects on the body, including improvedsleep, reduced inflammation, and enhanced immune function.

By practicing restorative yoga regularly, individuals can support their overall health and well-being, and cultivate a greater sense of peace and balance in their lives.

In conclusion, restorative yoga is a powerful practice for promoting relaxation and peace in today's fast-paced world. By focusing on gentle, restful poses and using props to support the body, individuals can experience a deep sense of relaxation and rejuvenation that can have a lasting impact on their overall well-being.

 Whether you are looking to reduce stress, improve sleep, or cultivate a greater sense of mindfulness, restorative yoga can offer a supportive and nurturing space to help you find peace and relaxation in your daily life. So why not give it a try and see how restorative yoga can help you on your journey to greater peace and well-being.

Chapter 2: Sleep Soundly with Restorative Yoga: A Step-by-Step

Sleep is a crucial aspect of our overall health and well-being, yet many of us struggle to get a good night's rest. From stress and anxiety to physical discomfort and insomnia, there are many factors that can disrupt our sleeppatterns. One effective way to promote better sleep is through the practice of restorative yoga.

Restorative yoga is a gentle and calming form of yoga that focuses on relaxation and deep breathing. By incorporating restorative yoga into your bedtime routine, you can help calm your mind, release tension in your body, and prepare yourself for a restful night of sleep.

In this step-by-step guide, we will explore how to practice restorative yoga for better sleep.

Step 1: Create a Relaxing Environment

The first step in practicing restorative yoga for better sleep is to create a relaxing environment in which to practice. Find a quiet and comfortable space in your home where you can lay out a yoga mat or a soft blanket.

Dim the lights, play some calming music, and light a candle or use essential oils to create a peaceful atmosphere.

Step 2: Begin with Deep Breathing

Once you have set the scene for your restorative yoga practice, begin by focusing on your breath. Sit or lie down on your mat with your eyes closed and take a few deep breaths in and out through your nose. Feel your belly riseand fall with each breath, and allow yourself to relax into the present moment.

As you continue to breathe deeply, bring your awareness to any tension or discomfort in your body. With each exhale, imagine releasing this tension and allowing yourself to sink deeper into relaxation.

Step 3: Practice Gentle Yoga Poses

After a few minutes of deep breathing, begin to move into gentle yoga poses that will help release tension in your body and prepare you for sleep. Some restorative yoga poses that are particularly beneficial for promotingbetter sleep include:

- Child's Pose: Begin on your hands and knees, then slowly lower your hips back towards your heels while reaching your arms forward. Rest your forehead on the mat and breathe deeply into your back body.

- Legs-Up-the-Wall Pose: Sit with your side against a wall and extend your legs up the wall. Allow your arms to rest by your sides and close your eyes as you breathe deeply into your belly.

- Supported Bridge Pose: Lie on your back with your knees bent and feet hip-width apart. Place a yoga block or cushion under your sacrum and allow your arms to rest by your sides. Close your eyes and focus on your breath as you relax into the pose.

- Reclining Bound Angle Pose: Lie on your back with the soles of your feet together and knees falling open to the sides. Place a cushion or bolster under your knees for support and allow your arms to rest by your sides.
Close your eyes and breathe deeply into your belly. Step 4: Stay

in Each Pose for Several Minutes

As you move through each restorative yoga pose, be sure to stay in each pose for several minutes to allow your body to fully relax and release tension. Focus on your breath and try to let go of any thoughts or worries that may be keeping you awake.

If you find that a particular pose is uncomfortable or causing pain, gently come out of the pose and modify it as needed. Remember that restorative yoga is meant to be gentle and nurturing, so listen to your body and only do what feels good for you.

Step 5: End with Savasana

After you have moved through a series of restorative yoga poses, end your practice with Savasana, or Corpse Pose. Lie on your back with your arms by your sides and palms facing up, allowing your body to completely relax into the mat. Close your eyes and focus on your breath as you surrender to the present moment.

Savasana is a powerful pose for promoting deep relaxation and preparing your body and mind for sleep. Stay in Savasana for at least 5-10 minutes, allowing yourself to fully let go and release any remaining tension or stress.

Step 6: Practice Mindfulness and Gratitude

As you finish your restorative yoga practice, take a few moments to practice mindfulness and gratitude. Bring your awareness to the present moment and notice how your body feels after your practice. Take a few deep breaths and express gratitude for the time you have taken to care for yourself and promote better sleep.

You may also want to set an intention or affirmation for a restful night of sleep. Repeat a positive affirmation such as "I am calm and peaceful" or "I am ready for a restful night of sleep" to help calm your mind and prepare yourself for bedtime.

Step 7: Maintain a Consistent Bedtime Routine

In addition to practicing restorative yoga for better sleep, it is important to maintain a consistent bedtime routine to support healthy sleep patterns.

The Ultimate Guide to Restorative Yoga for Deep, Restorative Sleep

Restorative yoga is a gentle form of yoga that focuses on relaxation and deep rest. It is a practice that can help you unwind, release tension, and prepare your body and mind for a restful night's sleep.

In this ultimate guide, we will explore the benefits of restorative yoga for deep, restorative sleep, as well as provide you with a step-by- step guide on how to incorporate restorative yoga into your bedtime routine.

The Importance of Deep, Restorative Sleep

Before we delve into the world of restorative yoga, let's first understand the importance of deep, restorative sleep. Sleep is essential for our overall health and well-being, as it allows our bodies to rest and repair, our minds to recharge, and our emotions to stabilize.

Without adequate sleep, we may experience a range of negative effects, including fatigue, irritability, poor concentration, and even an increased risk of developing chronic health conditions.

Deep, restorative sleep is particularly important for our

physical and mental health. During deep sleep, our bodies undergo essential processes such as muscle repair, hormone regulation, and memory consolidation. Without deep sleep, we may not fully benefit from these processes, leading to a range of health issues including weakened immune function, increased stress levels, and impaired cognitive function.

Restorative Yoga: A Path to Deep, Restorative Sleep

Restorative yoga is a form of yoga that focuses on relaxation, gentle stretching, and deep breathing. It is a practice that encourages you to slow down, release tension, and connect with your breath and body.

 By incorporating restorative yoga into your bedtime routine, you can create a sense of calm and relaxation that canhelp you prepare for a restful night's sleep.

The benefits of restorative yoga for deep, restorative sleep are numerous. By practicing restorative yoga beforebed, you can:

1. Reduce stress and anxiety: Restorative yoga encourages you to slow down, relax, and release tension from your body. By focusing on your breath and gentle movements, you can calm your mind and reduce stress andanxiety levels, making it easier to drift off to sleep.

2. Improve flexibility and mobility: Restorative yoga involves gentle stretching and movement, which can help improve

flexibility and mobility in your muscles and joints. By releasing tension and tightness in your body, you can create a sense of ease and comfort that can promote a deeper, more restorative sleep.

3. Enhance relaxation and mindfulness: Restorative yoga encourages you to be present in the moment, focusing on your breath and body sensations. By cultivating a sense of mindfulness and relaxation, you can quiet your mind, reduce racing thoughts, and create a peaceful environment that is conducive to deep, restorative sleep.

4. Promote physical and mental well-being: Restorative yoga can help improve your overall physical and mental well-being by reducing stress, improving sleep quality, and promoting relaxation.

By incorporating restorative yoga into your bedtime routine, you can create a sense of balance and harmony that can support your overall health and well-being.

How to Incorporate Restorative Yoga into Your Bedtime Routine

Now that you understand the benefits of restorative yoga for deep, restorative sleep, let's explore how you can incorporate this practice into your bedtime routine. Follow these steps to create a restorative yoga practice that can help you unwind, relax, and prepare for a restful night's sleep:

1. Set the mood: Create a peaceful and calming environment in your bedroom by dimming the lights, lighting a scented candle, and playing soft music. This will help you relax and unwind before beginning your restorative yoga practice.

2. Choose comfortable clothing: Wear loose, comfortable clothing that allows you to move freely and breathedeeply. This will help you feel relaxed and at ease during your practice.

3. Gather props: Gather props such as bolsters, blankets, and pillows to support your body in restorative yoga poses. These props can help you relax and release tension in your muscles, allowing you to fully benefit from thepractice.

4. Practice deep breathing: Begin your restorative yoga practice by focusing on your breath. Take slow, deep breaths in and out through your nose, allowing your breath to guide your movements and create a sense of calmand relaxation.

5. Start with gentle stretches: Start your restorative yoga practice with gentle stretches to release tension in yourmuscles and prepare your body for deeper relaxation. Focus on areas of tension such as your neck, shoulders, and lower back, moving slowly and mindfully through each stretch.

6. Hold restorative poses: Hold restorative yoga poses for several minutes, allowing your body to relax and release

tension. Use props such as bolsters and blankets to support your body in each pose, creating a sense of comfort and ease that can promote deep, restorative sleep.

Focus on relaxation: As you move through your restorative yoga practice, focus on relaxation and release.

Restorative Yoga: Your Ticket to a Restful Night's Sleep

Restorative yoga is a gentle and relaxing form of yoga that focuses on deep relaxation and stress relief. It is the perfect practice for those looking to unwind and rejuvenate both the body and mind.

In today's fast-paced world,many people struggle with getting a good night's sleep. Restorative yoga can be a powerful tool to help combat insomnia and improve the quality of your sleep.

Restorative yoga is a practice that involves holding gentle yoga poses for an extended period of time, typically 5-10 minutes or longer.

The poses are supported with props such as blankets, bolsters, and blocks to allow the body to fully relax and release tension.

This support helps to activate the parasympathetic nervous system, which is responsible for the body's rest and digest response. By activating this system, restorative yoga helps to calm themind, reduce stress, and promote relaxation.

One of the key benefits of restorative yoga is its ability to help regulate the body's stress response. When we are stressed, the body releases cortisol, a hormone that can disrupt sleep patterns and lead to insomnia. By practicing restorative yoga regularly, you can help to lower cortisol levels and promote a sense of calm and relaxation. This can have a profound impact on your ability to fall asleep and stay asleep throughout the night.

Restorative yoga can also help to release tension and tightness in the body, which can contribute to sleep disturbances. Many people carry tension in their shoulders, neck, and back, which can make it difficult to relax and unwind before bed.

By practicing restorative yoga, you can release this tension and create a sense of ease and comfort in the body. This can help you to drift off to sleep more easily and stay asleep throughout the night.

In addition to its physical benefits, restorative yoga also has a powerful impact on the mind. The practice encourages mindfulness and presence, helping you to let go of racing thoughts and worries that can keep you up at night.

By focusing on the breath and the sensations in the body, you can cultivate a sense of inner peace and quiet the mind. This can help you to let go of stress and anxiety, allowing you to fall into a deep and restful sleep.

To practice restorative yoga for better sleep, it is important to create a calming and peaceful environment. Find a quiet space where you won't be disturbed, and gather any props you may need for the practice.

You can use blankets, bolsters, pillows, and blocks to support your body in the poses. Wear comfortable clothing that allows you to move freely and breathe deeply.

Start by taking a few minutes to center yourself and connect with your breath. Close your eyes and take slow, deep breaths in and out through the nose. Allow your body to relax and soften with each exhale. Once you feel grounded and present, you can begin your restorative yoga practice.

One of the most common restorative yoga poses for better sleep is Legs-Up-The-Wall pose. To practice this pose, find a clear wall space and sit with your side against the wall.

Swing your legs up the wall and lie back on the floor, creating an L-shape with your body. You can place a bolster or blanket under your hips for support, and a pillow under your head for added comfort.

Close your eyes and breathe deeply, allowing your body to relax and release tension. Stay in this pose for 5-10 minutes, focusing on the sensation of your breath and the support of the wall.

Another restorative yoga pose for better sleep is Supported

Child's Pose. To practice this pose, place a bolster or pillow lengthwise on your mat and kneel in front of it. Sit back on your heels and fold forward, resting your torso on the bolster. You can place a blanket under your forehead for support, and a blanket or pillow under your thighs for added comfort. Close your eyes and breathe deeply, allowing your body to release tension and soften with each exhale. Stay in this pose for 5-10 minutes, focusing on the sensation of your breath and the support ofthe bolster.

Corpse pose, also known as Savasana, is another restorative yoga pose that can help promote better sleep. To practice this pose, lie on your back with your legs extended and your arms by your sides.

Close your eyes and allow your body to relax completely, releasing tension from head to toe. You can place a blanket under your head and a bolster under your knees for support. Focus on the sensation of your breath and the feeling of relaxation in your body. Stay in this pose for 5-10 minutes, allowing yourself to drift off into a peaceful andrestful sleep.

In addition to these poses, there are many other restorative yoga practices that can help promote better sleep. Gentle twists, forward folds, and side stretches can all help to release tension and create a sense of ease in thebody. By incorporating these poses into your bedtime routine,

Chapter 3: Relax, Restore, and Rejuvenate: Restorative Yoga for Better Sleep

Restorative yoga is a gentle and relaxing form of yoga that focuses on deep relaxation and rejuvenation. It is the perfect practice for those looking to unwind, de-stress, and improve their sleep quality.

In today's fast-paced world, many people struggle with getting a good night's sleep. Whether it's due to stress, anxiety, or simply an overactive mind, sleep is essential for our overall health and well-being. Restorative yoga can help promote better sleep by calming the mind and relaxing the body.

Restorative yoga is all about slowing down and taking the time to relax and restore the body. Unlike more vigorous forms of yoga, restorative yoga involves holding gentle poses for an extended period of time, allowing the body to fully relax and release tension.

 This practice is perfect for those who are looking to reduce stress, improve flexibility, and promote a sense of well-being.

One of the key benefits of restorative yoga is its ability to calm the nervous system and reduce stress. By focusing on deep breathing and gentle stretching, restorative yoga helps to activate the body's relaxation response, which can help lower cortisol levels and promote a sense of calm and peace. This can be especially beneficial for those who struggle with anxiety or insomnia, as restorative yoga can help quiet the mind and promote a more restful night's sleep.

In addition to reducing stress, restorative yoga can also help improve flexibility and range of motion. Many of the poses in restorative yoga are designed to gently stretch and release tension in the muscles, helping to improveflexibility and reduce stiffness.

This can be especially beneficial for those who spend long hours sitting at a desk or engaging in repetitive movements, as restorative yoga can help counteract the effects of a sedentary lifestyle and promote better overall physical health.

Another key benefit of restorative yoga is its ability to promote a sense of well-being and relaxation.

By taking the time to slow down and focus on the breath, restorative yoga can help quiet the mind and promote a sense ofinner peace.

This can be especially beneficial for those who struggle with racing thoughts or anxiety, as restorative yoga can help cultivate a sense of mindfulness and presence in the moment.

One of the best times to practice restorative yoga is before bed. By incorporating restorative yoga into your evening routine, you can help prepare your body and mind for a restful night's sleep. Restorative yoga can helprelax the body and calm the mind, making it easier to drift off to sleep and stay asleep throughout the night. By practicing restorative yoga regularly, you can help improve your sleep quality and wake up feeling refreshed andrejuvenated.

Here are some restorative yoga poses that are perfect for promoting better sleep:

1. Legs up the wall pose (Viparita Karani): This pose is a gentle inversion that can help promote relaxation and reduce stress. Simply lie on your back with your legs extended up the wall, keeping your hips close to the wall.Close your eyes and focus on deep, slow breathing, allowing the body to fully relax and release tension.

2. Child's pose (Balasana): This pose is a gentle stretch for the back and hips that can help promote relaxation and calm the mind. Begin on your hands and knees, then sit back on your heels and extend your arms forward, resting your forehead on the mat. Close your eyes and focus on deep breathing, allowing the body to release tension and unwind.

3. Supported bridge pose: This pose is a gentle backbend that

can help open the chest and promote relaxation. Lie on your back with your knees bent and feet flat on the floor, then place a yoga block or bolster under your sacrum for support. Close your eyes and focus on deep breathing, allowing the body to relax and release tension.

4. Reclining bound angle pose (Supta Baddha Konasana): This pose is a gentle hip opener that can help promoterelaxation and reduce stress. Lie on your back with the soles of your feet together and knees out to the sides, then place a bolster or pillow under your knees for support. Close your eyes and focus on deep breathing, allowing the body to fully relax and unwind.

5. Corpse pose (Savasana): This pose is a classic relaxation pose that can help promote deep relaxation and rejuvenation.

Simply lie on your back with your arms and legs extended, palms facing up. Close your eyes and focus on deep, slow breathing, allowing the body to fully relax and release tension.

Incorporating these restorative yoga poses into your evening routine can help promote better sleep and improve your overall well-being.

By taking the time to slow down and relax, you can help prepare your body and mind for a restful night's sleep. Whether you're dealing with stress, anxiety, or simply looking to improve your sleep quality, restorative yoga can be a powerful tool for relaxation and rejuvenation.

Sleep Better Tonight with Restorative Yoga: A Comprehensive Guide

Sleep is an essential aspect of our overall health and well-being. It is during sleep that our bodies repair and regenerate, allowing us to wake up feeling refreshed and ready to take on the day.

However, many people struggle with getting a good night's sleep, whether it be due to stress, anxiety, or other factors.

Restorative yoga is a gentle and relaxing practice that can help improve the quality of your sleep and promote a sense of calm and relaxation. In this comprehensive guide, we will explore how restorative yoga can help you sleep better tonight.

What is Restorative Yoga?

Restorative yoga is a form of yoga that focuses on relaxation and stress relief. It involves holding gentle poses for an extended period of time, usually with the support of props such as blankets, bolsters, and blocks.

The goal of restorative yoga is to activate the parasympathetic nervous system, also known as the "rest and digest" system, which helps the body relax and unwind.

Restorative yoga is a great practice for those who are looking to reduce stress, improve sleep, and promote overall well-being. It is accessible to people of all fitness levels and can be modified to suit individual needs andabilities.

How Restorative Yoga Can Help You Sleep Better

Restorative yoga can help improve the quality of your sleep in a number of ways. Here are some of the key benefits of incorporating restorative yoga into your bedtime routine:

1. Stress Relief: Restorative yoga is a great way to unwind and let go of the stress and tension that has built upthroughout the day. By focusing on deep breathing and gentle stretching, you can calm your mind and body,making it easier to fall asleep and stay asleep throughout the night.

2. Relaxation: The gentle, supported poses of restorative yoga help to relax the muscles and release tension in thebody. This can help promote a sense of deep relaxation and prepare your body for a restful night's sleep.

3. Improved Circulation: Restorative yoga poses can help improve circulation in the body, which can aid in therelease of toxins and promote better overall health. Better circulation can also help regulate body temperature, making it easier to fall asleep and stay asleep throughout the night.

4. Mindfulness: Restorative yoga encourages mindfulness and presence in the moment. By focusing on your breath and the sensations in your body, you can quiet the chatter of your mind and create a sense of calm and peace that can carry over into your sleep.

5. Hormone Regulation: Restorative yoga can help regulate the production of hormones such as cortisol, which isoften elevated in times of stress. By reducing cortisol levels through relaxation and deep breathing, you can create a more balanced hormonal environment that is conducive to restful sleep.

How to Practice Restorative Yoga for Better Sleep

If you are looking to improve the quality of your sleep with restorative yoga, here are some tips to help you getstarted:

1. Create a Relaxing Environment: Find a quiet, comfortable space where you can practice restorative yoga without distractions. Dim the lights, play soft music, and light a candle or diffuse essential oils to create a calming atmosphere.

2. Gather Your Props: You will need a few props to support you in your restorative yoga practice, such as blankets, bolsters, blocks, and pillows. These props will help you get into the poses comfortably and stay therefor an extended period of time.

3. Choose Poses that Promote Relaxation: There are many restorative yoga poses that can help promote relaxation and better sleep. Some of the most popular poses include Legs-Up-The-Wall Pose, Supported Child's Pose, and Reclining Bound Angle Pose. Choose poses that feel good in your body and allow you to relax deeply.

4. Focus on Your Breath: Throughout your restorative yoga practice, focus on your breath and try to cultivate slow, deep breathing. This will help activate the parasympathetic nervous system and promote relaxation in the body.

5. Practice Mindfulness: As you move through your restorative yoga practice, try to stay present in the moment and pay attention to the sensations in your body. This mindfulness can help quiet the mind and create a sense of calm that can carry over into your sleep.

6. Set a Bedtime Routine: Incorporate restorative yoga into your bedtime routine to signal to your body that it is time to wind down and prepare for sleep. Practice your restorative yoga poses for 15-20 minutes before bed to help relax your body and mind.

7. Be Consistent: Like any practice, consistency is key when it comes to reaping the benefits of restorative yoga for better sleep. Try to practice restorative yoga regularly, whether it be daily or a few times a week, to see improvements in your sleep

quality over time.

The Science of Sleep: How Restorative Yoga Can Help You Snooze

Sleep is an essential part of our daily routine, yet many of us struggle to get the rest we need. Whether it's due to stress, anxiety, or simply a busy schedule, sleep deprivation can have a serious impact on our physical and mentalhealth.

That's where restorative yoga comes in. This gentle form of yoga is specifically designed to help relax the body and mind, making it easier to fall asleep and stay asleep throughout the night.

Restorative yoga is a practice that focuses on relaxation and rejuvenation. It involves holding gentle poses for an extended period of time, allowing the body to fully relax and release tension.

Unlike more active forms of yoga, restorative yoga does not involve strenuous movements or intense physical exertion. Instead, it is about slowing down, tuning into the breath, and letting go of stress and tension.

One of the key benefits of restorative yoga is its ability to activate the body's parasympathetic nervous system, also known as the "rest and digest" system.

This system is responsible for helping the body relax and

unwind, promoting feelings of calm and tranquility. By engaging the parasympathetic nervous system through restorative yoga, we can help reduce levels of the stress hormone cortisol in the body, leading to a greater sense of relaxation and ease.

In addition to reducing stress and promoting relaxation, restorative yoga can also help improve sleep quality. By releasing tension in the body and calming the mind, restorative yoga can create the ideal conditions for a restfulnight's sleep.

Research has shown that regular practice of restorative yoga can help improve sleep patterns, reduce the time it takes to fall asleep, and increase overall sleep quality.

One of the reasons why restorative yoga is so effective for improving sleep is its focus on mindfulness and breath awareness.

By tuning into the breath and being fully present in the moment, we can quiet the mind and let go of racing thoughts that can keep us awake at night.

This mindfulness practice can help us cultivate a sense of inner peace and calm that carries over into our sleep, making it easier to drift off and stay asleep throughout thenight.

In addition to its physical and mental benefits, restorative yoga can also help improve our overall well-being. By promoting relaxation and reducing stress, restorative yoga can help lower blood pressure, improve immune function, and boost mood.

These benefits can have a ripple effect on our health, leading to greater vitality and asense of well-being in our daily lives.

So how can you incorporate restorative yoga into your bedtime routine to help improve your sleep? Here are afew simple tips to get you started:

1. Create a calming environment: Set the stage for a restful night's sleep by creating a peaceful and relaxing environment in your bedroom. Dim the lights, play soothing music, and light a scented candle to create a senseof tranquility.

2. Practice gentle poses: Before bed, try incorporating a few gentle restorative yoga poses into your routine. Poses like Child's Pose, Legs-Up-The-Wall, and Reclining Bound Angle Pose can help release tension in thebody and calm the mind, making it easier to fall asleep.

3. Focus on the breath: As you move through your restorative yoga practice, focus on your breath. Take slow, deep breaths in and out through the nose, allowing the breath to guide you into a state of relaxation and ease.

4. Let go of tension: As you hold each pose, consciously release tension in the body. Soften the muscles, relax the jaw,

and let go of any tightness or stiffness you may be holding onto. Allow yourself to fully surrender to the pose and the present moment.

5. Practice gratitude: Before bed, take a few moments to reflect on the day and express gratitude for the blessings in your life. Cultivating a sense of gratitude can help shift your focus from worries and anxieties to the positive aspects of your life, promoting a sense of peace and contentment.

By incorporating restorative yoga into your bedtime routine, you can create the ideal conditions for a restful night's sleep. By promoting relaxation, reducing stress, and cultivating mindfulness, restorative yoga can help improve sleep quality and overall well-being.

So next time you find yourself tossing and turning at night, why not roll out your yoga mat and give restorative yoga a try? Your body and mind will thank you for it.

Chapter 4: Restorative Yoga Poses to Help You Drift Off into Dreamland

Restorative yoga is a gentle and calming practice that focuses on relaxation and stress relief. It involves holding poses for an extended period of time, allowing the body to fully relax and release tension.

Restorative yoga is especially beneficial for those who struggle with insomnia or have trouble falling asleep. By incorporating restorative yoga poses into your bedtime routine, you can help calm your mind and body, making it easier to drift off into dreamland.

Here are some restorative yoga poses that can help you relax and prepare for a restful night's sleep:

1. Supported Child's Pose (Balasana)
   To begin, place a bolster or a stack of pillows on your mat. Kneel on the mat with your big toes touching and knees wide apart. Slowly lower your torso onto the bolster, resting your forehead on the mat or a pillow.

   Extend your arms out in front of you or alongside your body. Close your eyes and focus on your breath, allowing your body to relax and release tension.

2. Legs-Up-The-Wall Pose (Viparita Karani)
Find a clear wall space and sit with your right side against the wall. Swing your legs up the wall as you lower yourback onto the mat. You can place a bolster or pillow under your hips for added support. Extend your arms out to the sides with palms facing up.

Close your eyes and focus on your breath as you relax into this pose. Legs-Up- The-Wall Pose is a gentle inversion that can help calm the nervous system and promote relaxation.

3. Supported Bridge Pose (Setu Bandha Sarvangasana)
Lie on your back with your knees bent and feet hip-width apart. Place a bolster or a stack of pillows under your sacrum for support. Rest your arms at your sides with palms facing up.

Close your eyes and focus on your breath as you allow your body to relax into the bolster. Supported Bridge Pose helps open the chest and release tension in the spine, making it easier to breathe deeply and relax.

4. Reclining Bound Angle Pose (Supta Baddha Konasana)
Lie on your back with your knees bent and feet together. Allow your knees to fall open to the sides, bringing the soles of your feet together.

Place a bolster or pillows under your knees for support. Rest your arms at your sides with palms facing up. Close your eyes

and focus on your breath as you relax into this gentle hip opener.
Reclining Bound Angle Pose helps release tension in the hips and groin, promoting relaxation and deepbreathing.

5. Supported Corpse Pose (Savasana)
Lie on your back with your legs extended and arms at your sides. Place a bolster or pillows under your knees for support. Close your eyes and focus on your breath as you relax into this pose.

Supported Corpse Pose is a deeply relaxing pose that allows your body to fully relax and release tension. It can help calm the mind and prepare youfor a restful night's sleep.

Incorporating these restorative yoga poses into your bedtime routine can help you relax and unwind, making iteasier to drift off into dreamland.

Remember to focus on your breath and allow your body to fully relax in eachpose. By practicing restorative yoga regularly, you can improve your sleep quality and overall well-being. Give these poses a try and experience the benefits of restorative yoga for a peaceful night's sleep.

Say Goodnight to Insomnia with Restorative Yoga

Do you struggle with falling asleep or staying asleep at night? Do you find yourself tossing and turning for hourson end, unable to quiet your mind and relax your body? If so, you are not alone. Insomnia affects millions of people worldwide and can have a significant impact on your overall health and well-being.

One effective way to combat insomnia and improve your sleep quality is through the practice of restorative yoga. Restorative yoga is a gentle and relaxing form of yoga that focuses on deep relaxation and stress relief.

By incorporating restorative yoga into your bedtime routine, you can calm your mind, release tension in your body, and prepare yourself for a restful night's sleep.

In this article, we will explore the benefits of restorative yoga for insomnia and provide you with a simple bedtime yoga sequence to help you say goodnight to insomnia once and for all.

The Benefits of Restorative Yoga for Insomnia

Restorative yoga is a powerful tool for combating insomnia because it helps to activate the body's relaxation response.

When we are stressed or anxious, our bodies go into fight-or-flight mode, releasing stress hormones like cortisol that can interfere with our ability to fall asleep and stay asleep.

Restorative yoga works by activating the parasympathetic nervous system, which is responsible for promoting relaxation and rest. By engaging in gentle, supported poses and focusing on deep, mindful breathing, restorative yoga helps to calm the mind, reduce stress levels, and promote a sense of peace and tranquility.

In addition to promoting relaxation, restorative yoga can also help to release tension in the body. Many of us carry stress and tension in our muscles, particularly in areas like the neck, shoulders, and lower back.

By practicing restorative yoga poses that target these areas, you can release tightness and stiffness, allowing your body to fully relax and prepare for sleep.

Another benefit of restorative yoga for insomnia is its ability to improve circulation and digestion. When we are stressed, our bodies can become tense and constricted, leading to poor circulation and digestion. By practicing restorative yoga poses that open up the chest, shoulders, and hips, you can improve blood flow and stimulate the digestive system, helping to promote a sense of ease and relaxation.

Overall, restorative yoga is a gentle and effective way to

combat insomnia and improve your sleep quality. By incorporating restorative yoga into your bedtime routine, you can create a peaceful and calming environment that will help you drift off to sleep and wake up feeling refreshed and rejuvenated.

A Bedtime Yoga Sequence for Insomnia

If you are struggling with insomnia and looking for a natural way to improve your sleep quality, try incorporating the following bedtime yoga sequence into your nightly routine. This sequence is designed to help you relax your mind and body, release tension, and prepare yourself for a restful night's sleep.

1. Child's Pose (Balasana)

Start by kneeling on the floor with your big toes touching and your knees hip-width apart. Sit back on your heels and fold forward, reaching your arms out in front of you. Rest your forehead on the mat and take a few deep breaths, focusing on relaxing your body and quieting your mind.

Child's Pose is a gentle and soothing pose that helps to release tension in the back, shoulders, and neck. It also promotes a sense of calm and relaxation, making it an ideal pose to start your bedtime yoga sequence.

2. Legs Up the Wall Pose (Viparita Karani)

Lie on your back with your hips close to a wall. Extend your legs up the wall, keeping them straight and relaxed. Rest your arms by your sides with your palms facing up. Close your eyes and focus on your breath, allowing your body to relax and release tension.

Legs Up the Wall Pose is a restorative pose that helps to improve circulation and reduce swelling in the legs and feet. It also helps to calm the nervous system and promote relaxation, making it an excellent pose for preparing your body for sleep.

3. Reclining Bound Angle Pose (Supta Baddha Konasana)

Lie on your back with your knees bent and the soles of your feet together. Allow your knees to fall open to the sides, creating a diamond shape with your legs.

Place your hands on your belly or let them rest by your sides. Close your eyes and take deep, slow breaths, allowing your body to relax and release tension.

Reclining Bound Angle Pose is a gentle hip opener that helps to release tension in the hips, groin, and lower back. It also helps to calm the mind and promote a sense of peace and tranquility, making it an excellent pose for preparing for sleep.

Restorative Yoga for Sleep: A Holistic Approach to Better Rest

Restorative yoga is a gentle form of yoga that focuses on relaxation and rejuvenation. It is a holistic approach to better rest that can help improve sleep quality and overall well-being.

In today's fast-paced world, many people struggle with sleep issues due to stress, anxiety, and other factors. Restorative yoga offers a natural and effective way to promote relaxation and help the body and mind unwind before bedtime.

Restorative yoga involves holding gentle poses for an extended period of time, typically 5-10 minutes or longer. These poses are supported by props such as bolsters, blankets, and blocks to help the body relax and release tension.

The practice also includes deep breathing techniques and mindfulness meditation to help calm the mind and promote a sense of inner peace.

One of the key benefits of restorative yoga is its ability to activate the parasympathetic nervous system, also known as the "rest and digest" system. This helps to counteract the effects of the sympathetic nervous system, which is responsible for the body's stress response.

By activating the parasympathetic nervous system, restorative yoga can help reduce stress levels, lower blood pressure, and promote relaxation, making it an ideal practice for improving sleep quality.

Research has shown that restorative yoga can be an effective tool for improving sleep. A study published in the Journal of Alternative and Complementary Medicine found that participants who practiced restorative yoga experienced significant improvements in sleep quality, including reduced sleep disturbances and increased sleep efficiency.

Another study published in the Journal of Clinical Sleep Medicine found that restorative yoga was effective in reducing symptoms of insomnia and improving overall sleep quality in adults with chronic insomnia.

In addition to promoting relaxation and improving sleep quality, restorative yoga can also help reduce anxiety and improve mood.

A study published in the Journal of Alternative and Complementary Medicine found that participants who practiced restorative yoga experienced significant reductions in anxiety levels and improvements in mood.

Another study published in the Journal of Psychiatric Research found that restorative yoga was effective in reducing symptoms of depression and improving overall well-being in individuals with major depressive disorder.

Restorative yoga can be a valuable tool for anyone looking to improve their sleep and overall well-being. Whether you struggle with insomnia, stress, or anxiety, incorporating restorative yoga into your daily routine can help you relax, unwind, and prepare your body and mind for a restful night's sleep. Here are some tips for incorporating restorative yoga into your bedtime routine:

1. Create a peaceful environment: Find a quiet, comfortable space where you can practice restorative yoga without distractions. Dim the lights, play calming music, and light a candle or use essential oils to create a relaxing atmosphere.

2. Choose supportive props: Use props such as bolsters, blankets, and blocks to support your body in each pose. This will help you relax more deeply and release tension in your muscles.

3. Practice deep breathing: Focus on slow, deep breathing as you move through each pose. This will help calm your mind and activate the parasympathetic nervous system, promoting relaxation and restful sleep.

4. Stay present: Practice mindfulness meditation as you hold each pose. Focus on the sensations in your body, the

rhythm of your breath, and the present moment. This will help quiet your mind and reduce stress and anxiety.

5. Listen to your body: Pay attention to how each pose feels in your body. If a pose feels uncomfortable or painful, adjust your position or use more props to support yourself. Remember that restorative yoga is about relaxation, not straining or pushing yourself.

6. Practice regularly: Aim to incorporate restorative yoga into your bedtime routine at least a few times a week.Consistency is key to reaping the benefits of this practice and improving your sleep quality over time.

In conclusion, restorative yoga is a holistic approach to better rest that can help improve sleep quality, reduce stress and anxiety, and promote overall well-being.

By incorporating restorative yoga into your bedtime routine, you can create a peaceful and relaxing environment, support your body with props, practice deep breathing andmindfulness meditation, and listen to your body's needs.

With regular practice, you can experience the restorative benefits of this gentle form of yoga and enjoy a more restful and rejuvenating night's sleep.

Chapter 5: Transform Your Sleep with Restorative Yoga

Are you struggling to get a good night's sleep? Do you find yourself tossing and turning, unable to quiet your mind and relax your body? If so, restorative yoga may be just what you need to transform your sleep and improve your overall well-being.

Restorative yoga is a gentle, therapeutic form of yoga that focuses on relaxation and stress relief. It involves using props such as blankets, bolsters, and blocks to support the body in various poses, allowing you to completely relax and let go of tension. By practicing restorative yoga before bed, you can help calm your mind, release physical tension, and prepare your body for a restful night of sleep.

In this complete guide, we will explore the benefits of restorative yoga for sleep, as well as provide you with astep-by-step guide on how to incorporate it into your bedtime routine. By following these tips and techniques, you can transform your sleep and wake up feeling refreshed and rejuvenated each morning.

The Benefits of Restorative Yoga for Sleep

Restorative yoga offers a wide range of benefits for both the body and mind, making it an ideal practice for improving sleep quality. Some of the key benefits of restorative yoga for sleep include:

1. Stress Relief: Restorative yoga helps to activate the body's relaxation response, reducing levels of the stress hormone cortisol. By calming the nervous system and quieting the mind, restorative yoga can help you let go of the worries and anxieties that may be keeping you awake at night.

2. Muscle Relaxation: Many of us carry tension in our bodies, particularly in the neck, shoulders, and back. By using props to support the body in restorative yoga poses, you can release physical tension and tightness, allowing your muscles to relax and unwind.

3. Improved Circulation: Restorative yoga poses are designed to gently stretch and open the body, promoting better blood flow and circulation. This can help to reduce inflammation, improve oxygen flow to the muscles, and support the body's natural healing processes.

4. Enhanced Breathing: Deep, diaphragmatic breathing is a key component of restorative yoga. By focusing on slow, mindful breathing during your practice, you can calm the mind, reduce anxiety, and promote a sense of relaxation that can carry over into your sleep.

5. Mindfulness and Presence: Restorative yoga encourages

you to be fully present in the moment, tuning in to the sensations in your body and letting go of distractions. By cultivating mindfulness through your practice, you can quiet the chatter of the mind and create a sense of inner peace that can help you drift off to sleep more easily.

How to Practice Restorative Yoga for Sleep

Now that you understand the benefits of restorative yoga for sleep, let's explore how you can incorporate this practice into your bedtime routine. Follow these steps to create a restorative yoga practice that will help you relax, unwind, and prepare for a restful night of sleep:

1. Set the Scene: Create a peaceful, calming environment for your restorative yoga practice. Dim the lights, light

   a candle or diffuse essential oils, and play soft, soothing music to help you relax and unwind.

2. Gather Your Props: You will need a few props to support your body in restorative yoga poses. Some essential props to have on hand include a yoga mat, two blankets, a bolster or cushion, and two blocks. If you don't have these props, you can also use pillows, cushions, or towels as substitutes.

3. Begin with Gentle Movement: Start your restorative yoga practice with a few gentle movements to warm up the body and release any tension. You can begin by sitting or lying down and gently stretching the neck, shoulders, and back. Move slowly

and mindfully, focusing on your breath and allowing your body to relax.

4. Practice Supported Child's Pose: One of the most relaxing restorative yoga poses for sleep is Supported Child's Pose. To practice this pose, place a bolster or cushion on your mat and kneel in front of it. Sit back on your heels and then fold forward, resting your torso on the bolster and turning your head to one side. Stay in thispose for 5-10 minutes, focusing on deep, slow breathing and allowing your body to relax.

5. Try Legs-Up-the-Wall Pose: Another restorative yoga pose that can help you relax and unwind before bed is Legs-Up-the-Wall Pose. To practice this pose, place a blanket or cushion against the wall and sit with your side against the wall. Swing your legs up the wall and lie back, resting your head on the blanket. Stay in this pose for 5-10 minutes, focusing on your breath and allowing your body to release tension.

End with Savasana: Finish your restorative yoga practice with Savasana, or Corpse Pose. Lie on your back with your legs extended and your arms by your sides, palms facing up.

Restorative Yoga: Your Key to Deep, Restorative Sleep

Restorative yoga is a gentle form of yoga that focuses on relaxation and rejuvenation. It is a practice that allowsthe body to rest deeply and restore itself, promoting a sense of calm and well-being. Restorative yoga is particularly beneficial for those who struggle with sleep issues, as it can help to calm the mind and relax the body, making it easier to achieve deep, restorative sleep.

In today's fast-paced world, many people struggle with sleep problems. Whether it's difficulty falling asleep, staying asleep, or waking up feeling tired and groggy, sleep issues can have a significant impact on our overall health and well-being. Restorative yoga offers a natural and effective way to address these issues and improvethe quality of your sleep.

One of the key benefits of restorative yoga is its ability to activate the body's relaxation response. This response, also known as the parasympathetic nervous system, is responsible for slowing the heart rate, relaxing the muscles, and calming the mind.

By practicing restorative yoga, you can help to activate this response and promote a state of deep relaxation that is conducive to sleep.

In restorative yoga, poses are held for an extended period of time, typically 5-10 minutes or longer. This allows the body to fully relax and release tension, promoting a sense of ease and comfort. By holding poses for an extended period of time, you can also help to increase circulation and improve flexibility, which can further enhance the quality of your sleep.

Another key benefit of restorative yoga for sleep is its focus on mindful breathing. Deep, diaphragmatic breathing is a powerful tool for calming the mind and relaxing the body. By focusing on your breath during restorative yoga practice, you can help to quiet the mind and release any tension or stress that may be keepingyou awake at night.

In addition to promoting relaxation and calming the mind, restorative yoga can also help to alleviate physical discomfort that may be interfering with your sleep.

Many restorative yoga poses are designed to target specific areas of the body, such as the back, hips, and shoulders, where tension and tightness often accumulate. By releasing tension in these areas, you can help to reduce pain and discomfort, making it easier to relax and fall asleep.

Some restorative yoga poses that are particularly beneficial for sleep include:

- Legs up the wall: This pose involves lying on your back with your legs extended up against a wall. It can help to improve circulation, reduce swelling in the legs, and promote a sense of relaxation and calm.

- Supported child's pose: In this pose, you kneel on the floor with your knees apart and your forehead resting on a bolster or cushion. This pose can help to release tension in the back, shoulders, and hips, promoting a sense of ease and relaxation.

- Supported reclining bound angle pose: This pose involves lying on your back with the soles of your feet together and your knees apart, supported by bolsters or cushions. It can help to open the hips and release tension in the groin and lower back, promoting a sense of relaxation and ease.

- Supported savasana: Savasana, or corpse pose, is a classic relaxation pose that involves lying on your back with
your arms and legs extended and your eyes closed. By adding bolsters or cushions under the knees and head, you can help to support the body and promote a deeper sense of relaxation.

Incorporating restorative yoga into your bedtime routine can help to prepare your body and mind for sleep. By practicing a few gentle restorative poses before bed, you can help to release tension, calm the mind, and promote a sense of relaxation that is conducive to sleep. You can also use restorative yoga as a tool for managing stress and anxiety throughout the day, helping to create a sense of calm and ease that can carry over into your sleep.

In addition to practicing restorative yoga, there are several other strategies you can use to improve the quality of your sleep. These include:

- Establishing a consistent bedtime routine: Going to bed and waking up at the same time each day can help to regulate your body's internal clock and improve the quality of your sleep.

- Creating a relaxing sleep environment: Make sure your bedroom is dark, quiet, and cool, and consider using white noise or a sound machine to block out any distractions.

- Limiting screen time before bed: The blue light emitted by screens can interfere with your body's production of melatonin, a hormone that regulates sleep. Try to avoid screens for at least an hour before bed to help promote restful sleep.

- Practicing good sleep hygiene: Avoid caffeine, alcohol, and heavy meals close to bedtime, and try to engage in relaxing activities, such as reading or taking a warm bath, before bed.

Restorative Yoga: The Secret to a Peaceful Night's Rest

Restorative yoga is a gentle and relaxing form of yoga that focuses on deep relaxation and stress relief. It is the perfect practice for those looking to unwind and rejuvenate after a long day. Restorative yoga uses props such asblankets, bolsters, and blocks to support the body in various poses, allowing for a deeper sense of relaxation and release.

One of the key benefits of restorative yoga is its ability to promote a peaceful night's rest. By practicing restorative yoga before bed, you can help calm the mind, release tension in the body, and prepare yourself for arestful night's sleep.

In this article, we will explore the benefits of restorative yoga for sleep, as well as some simple poses you can try at home to help you relax and unwind before bedtime.

Restorative Yoga and Sleep

Restorative yoga is a powerful tool for promoting relaxation and reducing stress, both of which are essential for a good night's sleep.

When we are stressed or anxious, our bodies release cortisol, a hormone that can interfere with our ability to fall asleep and stay asleep. By practicing restorative yoga, we can help lower cortisol levels, calm the nervous system, and prepare the body and mind for sleep.

In addition to reducing stress, restorative yoga also helps release tension in the body. Many of us carry tension in our muscles, particularly in areas like the shoulders, neck, and lower back.

This tension can make it difficult to relax and fall asleep at night. By practicing restorative yoga, we can gently stretch and release these tense muscles, allowing for a greater sense of ease and relaxation in the body.

Restorative yoga also encourages deep breathing, which can help calm the mind and promote relaxation. When we are stressed or anxious, our breathing tends to be shallow and rapid, which can signal to the body that we arein a state of fight or flight.

By practicing deep, slow breathing in restorative yoga poses, we can signal to the body that it is safe to relax and unwind, helping us prepare for a peaceful night's rest.

Simple Restorative Yoga Poses for Sleep

If you are looking to incorporate restorative yoga into your bedtime routine, here are some simple poses you can try at home to help promote relaxation and prepare for sleep:

1.   Supported Child's Pose: Begin by placing a bolster or a stack of blankets on your mat. Kneel on the floor, then lower your chest and forehead onto the bolster or blankets. Extend your arms out in front of you or place them by your sides. Close your eyes and focus on your breath, allowing yourself to relax and release tension in the body.

2.   Legs-Up-the-Wall Pose: Sit with your right side against a wall, then swing your legs up the wall as you lie back on the floor. You can place a bolster or blanket under your hips for added support. Close your eyes and relax intothe pose, focusing on your breath and allowing your body to release tension and stress.

3.   Supported Reclining Bound Angle Pose: Sit on the floor with a bolster or stack of blankets behind you. Bringthe soles of your feet together and let your knees fall out to the sides.

 Lie back on the bolster or blankets, supporting your head and chest. Close your eyes and relax into the pose, focusing on your breath and allowingyourself to release tension in the hips and lower back.

4.   Supported Savasana: Lie on your back with a bolster or stack of blankets under your knees. Place a blanket oreye pillow over your eyes to help block out any light. Close your eyes and relax

into the pose, focusing on your breath and allowing yourself to release tension in the body.

Incorporating these simple restorative yoga poses into your bedtime routine can help promote relaxation, reduce stress, and prepare your body and mind for a peaceful night's rest. By taking the time to unwind and release tension before bed, you can create a sense of calm and ease that will help you fall asleep more easily and enjoy arestful night's sleep.

Tips for Practicing Restorative Yoga for Sleep

In addition to incorporating restorative yoga poses into your bedtime routine, there are some additional tips you can follow to help promote a peaceful night's rest:

1.   Create a Relaxing Environment: Set the mood for relaxation by dimming the lights, lighting candles or incense, and playing soft, soothing music. Creating a peaceful environment can help signal to your body that it is time to unwind and prepare for sleep.

2.   Practice Mindfulness: Before bed, take a few moments to practice mindfulness or meditation. Sit quietly and focus on your breath, allowing yourself to let go of any worries or stress from the day. By practicing mindfulness, you can help calm the mind and prepare yourself for a restful night's sleep.

Chapter 6: Sleep Like a Baby: Restorative Yoga Poses for Better Zzz's

Sleep is an essential part of our daily lives, yet many of us struggle to get the restful and rejuvenating sleep that our bodies and minds need.

Whether it's stress, anxiety, or simply an inability to relax, there are a multitude of factors that can interfere with our ability to fall asleep and stay asleep throughout the night. But fear not, there isa solution that can help you achieve the deep and restorative sleep you crave – restorative yoga.

Restorative yoga is a gentle and relaxing form of yoga that focuses on deep breathing, gentle stretching, and supported poses to help calm the mind and body.

By incorporating restorative yoga into your bedtime routine, you can create a peaceful and tranquil environment that promotes relaxation and prepares your body for sleep.

Inthis article, we will explore some restorative yoga poses that can help you sleep like a baby and wake up feeling refreshed and rejuvenated.

1. Child's Pose (Balasana)

Child's pose is a soothing and grounding pose that can help calm the mind and release tension in the body. To practice child's pose, start by kneeling on the floor with your big toes touching and your knees hip-width apart.

Sit back on your heels and then slowly lower your forehead to the floor, extending your arms out in front of you or resting them alongside your body. Take deep breaths in this pose, allowing your body to relax and release anytension or stress.

2. Legs-Up-The-Wall Pose (Viparita Karani)

Legs-up-the-wall pose is a restorative pose that helps to calm the nervous system and promote relaxation. To practice this pose, lie on your back with your hips close to a wall.

Extend your legs up the wall, keeping them straight or slightly bent if that is more comfortable. Rest your arms alongside your body with your palms facing up. Close your eyes and focus on your breath, allowing your body to relax and release any tension.

3. Reclining Bound Angle Pose (Supta Baddha Konasana)

Reclining bound angle pose is a gentle hip opener that can help release tension in the hips and groin area. To practice this pose, lie on your back with your knees bent and the soles of your feet together, allowing your knees to fall open to the sides. Place your hands on your belly or let them rest alongside your body. Close your eyes and focus on your breath, allowing your body to relax and release any tension in the hips and groin.

4. Supported Bridge Pose (Setu Bandhasana)

Supported bridge pose is a restorative pose that helps to open the chest and shoulders while also calming the mind. To practice this pose, lie on your back with your knees bent and your feet hip-width apart.

Place a yoga block or bolster underneath your sacrum and allow your hips to be supported by the prop. Rest your arms alongside your body with your palms facing up. Close your eyes and focus on your breath, allowing your body to relax and release any tension in the chest and shoulders.

5. Corpse Pose (Savasana)

Corpse pose is a classic relaxation pose that can help calm the mind and promote deep relaxation. To practice corpse pose, lie on your back with your legs extended and your arms resting alongside your body with your

palms facing up. Close your eyes and focus on your breath, allowing your body to relax completely. Stay in this pose for at least 5-10 minutes, allowing yourself to fully let go and surrender to the present moment.

Incorporating these restorative yoga poses into your bedtime routine can help you create a peaceful and tranquilenvironment that promotes relaxation and prepares your body for sleep. By focusing on deep breathing, gentle stretching, and supported poses, you can calm your mind and release tension in your body, allowing you to drift off to sleep easily and wake up feeling refreshed and rejuvenated.

In addition to practicing restorative yoga poses, there are several other tips and tricks that can help improve thequality of your sleep. Here are a few suggestions to help you sleep like a baby:

1. Create a bedtime routine: Establishing a consistent bedtime routine can help signal to your body that it is timeto wind down and prepare for sleep. Try to go to bed at the same time each night and engage in relaxing activities such as reading, meditating, or practicing restorative yoga before bed.

2. Limit screen time: The blue light emitted from screens can interfere with your body's natural sleep-wake cycle, making it difficult to fall asleep. Try to limit screen time at least an hour before bed and opt for activities that promote relaxation and calm.

3. Create a peaceful sleep environment: Make sure your bedroom is a peaceful and tranquil environment thatpromotes relaxation and restful sleep. Keep your room cool, dark, and

quiet, and consider using white noise machines or earplugs to block out any disruptive sounds.

The Art of Relaxation: Restorative Yoga for Better

In today's fast-paced world, many people struggle with stress and anxiety, leading to difficulty falling asleep and staying asleep.

The lack of quality sleep can have a significant impact on our overall health and well-being, affecting our mood, energy levels, and cognitive function. Fortunately, there are natural and effective ways to promote relaxation and improve sleep, one of which is restorative yoga.

Restorative yoga is a gentle and therapeutic form of yoga that focuses on relaxation and rejuvenation. It involves holding passive poses for an extended period of time, typically 5-10 minutes, using props such as blankets, bolsters, and blocks to support the body in a comfortable and restful position.

This allows the muscles to relax deeply, the nervous system to calm down, and the mind to quieten, promoting a state of deep relaxation and inner peace.

One of the key benefits of restorative yoga is its ability to activate the parasympathetic nervous system, also known as the "rest and digest" system.

This is the body's natural response to relaxation and helps to counteract the effects of the sympathetic nervous system, which is responsible for the "fight or flight" response to stress. By activating the parasympathetic nervous system through restorative yoga, we can reduce stress hormones such as cortisol, lower blood pressure, and promote a sense of calm and well-being, all of which are essential for a good night's sleep.

In addition to its physiological benefits, restorative yoga also has a profound impact on the mind and emotions. By practicing deep relaxation and mindfulness in restorative poses, we can release tension and negative emotions stored in the body, quieten the mind chatter, and cultivate a sense of inner peace and contentment.

This can helpto alleviate anxiety, depression, and other mental health issues that may be interfering with our ability to relax and sleep well.

So how can we incorporate restorative yoga into our daily routine to improve sleep quality? Here are some tips and techniques to help you get started:

1. Create a Relaxing Environment: To practice restorative yoga effectively, it's important to create a peaceful and quiet space where you can relax without distractions.

Choose a comfortable and warm room, dim the lights, and play soft music or nature sounds to enhance the ambiance. You may also want to use aromatherapy candles or essential oils such as lavender, chamomile, or sandalwood to promote relaxation and sleep.

2. Set Aside Time for Practice: Schedule a regular time each day to practice restorative yoga, ideally in the evening before bedtime.

This will help to signal to your body and mind that it's time to unwind and prepare forsleep. Aim to practice for at least 20-30 minutes, but feel free to extend the session if you're feeling particularlystressed or tense.

3. Choose Comfortable Props: Invest in high-quality yoga props such as bolsters, blankets, blocks, and eye pillows to support your body in restorative poses.

These props will help you to relax deeply, release tension, and maintain proper alignment without strain or discomfort. Experiment with different props and positions to find what works best for your body and needs.

4. Practice Deep Breathing: One of the key components of restorative yoga is deep breathing, which helps tocalm the nervous system, reduce stress, and promote relaxation.

Focus on slow, deep, and mindful breathing throughout your

practice, inhaling deeply through the nose and exhaling slowly through the mouth. This will help to oxygenate the body, release tension, and quieten the mind, preparing you for a restful night's sleep.

5. Relax in Supported Poses: Choose a few restorative poses that feel comfortable and soothing for your body, such as Supta Baddha Konasana (Reclining Bound Angle Pose), Balasana (Child's Pose), or Viparita Karani (Legs-Up-the-Wall Pose). Use props to support your body in these poses, allowing yourself to relax deeply and surrender to gravity. Hold each pose for 5-10 minutes or longer, focusing on your breath and sensations in the body.

6. Practice Yoga Nidra: Yoga Nidra, also known as yogic sleep, is a powerful relaxation technique that combines deep relaxation with guided meditation.

It involves lying down in a comfortable position and following a series of verbal instructions to relax the body, calm the mind, and enter a state of deep relaxation.

Yoga Nidra can help to release tension, reduce anxiety, and promote restful sleep, making it an excellent practice for improving sleep quality.

Cultivate Mindfulness: In addition to physical relaxation, restorative yoga also helps to cultivate mindfulness, or present-moment awareness.

Restorative Yoga: Your Pathway to Serene Sleep

Restorative yoga is a gentle and relaxing form of yoga that focuses on deep relaxation and stress relief. It is a practice that can help calm the mind, release tension in the body, and promote a sense of overall well-being.

Oneof the many benefits of restorative yoga is its ability to help improve sleep quality. In this article, we will explore how restorative yoga can be a pathway to serene sleep and how incorporating this practice into your daily routine can help you achieve a more restful and rejuvenating night's sleep.

Restorative yoga is a practice that involves holding gentle and supported yoga poses for an extended period of time. The use of props such as bolsters, blankets, and blocks helps to support the body in each pose, allowing fora deeper sense of relaxation and release.

By holding these poses for an extended period of time, restorative yogahelps to activate the parasympathetic nervous system, also known as the "rest and digest" system.

This activation helps to counteract the effects of the sympathetic nervous system, which is responsible for the body's "fight or flight" response to stress.

One of the key benefits of restorative yoga is its ability to help reduce stress and anxiety. By focusing on deep breathing and relaxation, restorative yoga can help calm the mind and release tension in the body.

This can be particularly helpful for those who struggle with insomnia or have difficulty falling asleep due to stress or anxiety. By incorporating restorative yoga into your daily routine, you can help to create a sense of calm and relaxation that can carry over into your sleep routine.

In addition to reducing stress and anxiety, restorative yoga can also help to improve circulation and digestion. Byholding gentle poses for an extended period of time, restorative yoga helps to improve blood flow and lymphaticdrainage, which can help to reduce inflammation and promote overall health.

Improved circulation can also helpto promote better sleep by ensuring that the body is able to relax and release tension more effectively.

Another benefit of restorative yoga is its ability to help improve flexibility and mobility. By holding gentle posesfor an extended period of time, restorative yoga can help to release tension in the muscles and joints, allowing for greater range of motion and flexibility.

This can be particularly helpful for those who suffer from

chronic pain or stiffness, as restorative yoga can help to alleviate tension and improve overall mobility. By incorporating restorative yoga into your daily routine, you can help to improve your overall physical health and well-being, which can in turn help to promote a more restful night's sleep.

One of the key principles of restorative yoga is the importance of mindfulness and presence.

By focusing on the breath and being present in the moment, restorative yoga can help to quiet the mind and promote a sense of innerpeace.

 This mindfulness practice can be particularly helpful for those who struggle with racing thoughts or insomnia, as it can help to calm the mind and create a sense of stillness and tranquility.

By incorporating restorative yoga into your daily routine, you can help to cultivate a sense of mindfulness and presence that can carry over into your sleep routine, helping you to achieve a more restful and rejuvenating night's sleep.

Incorporating restorative yoga into your daily routine can be a simple and effective way to improve your sleep quality and overall well-being. By taking the time to practice gentle and supported poses, you can help to release tension in the body, calm the mind, and promote a sense of relaxation and serenity.

Whether you are new to yogaor have been practicing for years, restorative yoga can be a valuable tool for improving your sleep and overall health.

If you are interested in incorporating restorative yoga into your daily routine, there are a few key tips to keep in mind. First, it is important to listen to your body and only practice poses that feel comfortable and supportive. Using props such as bolsters, blankets, and blocks can help to provide additional support and comfort in each pose, allowing you to relax and release tension more effectively.

Second, it is important to focus on the breath and be present in the moment during your practice. By paying attention to your breath and being mindful of your body, you can help to quiet the mind and promote a sense of inner peace and relaxation.

Finally, it is important to practice regularly and consistently in order to experience the full benefits of restorative yoga. By incorporating restorative yoga into your daily routine, you can help to create a sense of calm and relaxation that can carry over into your sleep routine, helping you to achieve a more restful and rejuvenating night's sleep.

In conclusion, restorative yoga can be a valuable pathway to serene sleep. By incorporating gentle and supported poses into your daily routine, you can help to release tension in the body, calm the mind, and promote a sense of relaxation and well-being. Whether you are new to yoga or have been practicing for years, restorative yoga can be a valuable

Chapter 7: Restorative Yoga for Better Sleep

In today's fast-paced world, many of us struggle to get a good night's sleep. Whether it's due to stress, anxiety, or simply not being able to unwind after a long day, sleep can often feel elusive.

Restorative yoga offers a gentle and effective way to relax the body and mind, promoting better sleep and overall well-being. This comprehensive workbook will guide you through a series of restorative yoga poses and practices designed to help you achieve a more restful and rejuvenating night's sleep.

Understanding Restorative Yoga

Restorative yoga is a form of yoga that focuses on relaxation and rejuvenation. Unlike more active styles of yoga, restorative yoga involves holding gentle poses for an extended period of time, allowing the body to fully relax and release tension. By using props such as blankets, bolsters, and blocks, restorative yoga supports the body in a way that encourages deep relaxation and stress relief.

In restorative yoga, the emphasis is on slowing down and tuning into the body's natural rhythms. By practicing restorative yoga regularly, you can learn to quiet the mind, reduce stress, and promote a sense of calm and well-being. This can be especially beneficial for those struggling with sleep issues, as restorative yoga can help to quiet the mind and prepare the body for a restful night's sleep.

Benefits of Restorative Yoga for Sleep

There are many benefits to practicing restorative yoga for better sleep. Some of the key benefits include:

1. Stress Reduction: Restorative yoga helps to activate the parasympathetic nervous system, which is responsible for the body's relaxation response. By promoting relaxation and reducing stress, restorative yoga can help to calmthe mind and prepare the body for sleep.

2. Improved Circulation: The gentle stretching and deep breathing techniques used in restorative yoga can help to improve circulation and promote relaxation. This can help to reduce muscle tension and promote a sense of calm and well-being, making it easier to fall asleep and stay asleep throughout the night.

3. Enhanced Mindfulness: Restorative yoga encourages mindfulness and present-moment awareness, helping youto let go of worries and distractions that can interfere with sleep. By focusing on the breath and the sensations in the body, you can learn to quiet the mind and prepare for a restful night's sleep.

4. Improved Sleep Quality: By promoting relaxation and stress reduction, restorative yoga can help to improve the quality of your sleep. This can lead to a more restful and rejuvenating night's sleep, leaving you feeling refreshed and energized in the morning.

Restorative Yoga Poses for Better Sleep

There are many restorative yoga poses that can help to promote better sleep. Some of the most effective poses include:

1. Supported Child's Pose: This pose helps to release tension in the back and shoulders, promoting relaxation and stress relief. To practice this pose, place a bolster or pillow on the floor and kneel in front of it, then lower your chest and forehead to the bolster, resting your arms by your sides.

2. Legs-Up-the-Wall Pose: This pose helps to promote relaxation and reduce stress by allowing the legs to rest against a wall, promoting circulation and calming the nervous system. To practice this pose, lie on your back with your legs extended up a wall, keeping your hips and shoulders on the floor.

3. Supported Bridge Pose: This pose helps to open the chest and shoulders, promoting deep breathing and relaxation. To practice this pose, lie on your back with your knees bent and feet hip-width apart, then lift your hips and place a block or

bolster under your sacrum.

4. Reclining Bound Angle Pose: This pose helps to open the hips and release tension in the groin and inner thighs, promoting relaxation and stress relief. To practice this pose, lie on your back with the soles of your feet together and knees falling open, supporting your knees with blocks or bolsters if needed.

Creating a Restorative Yoga Routine for Better Sleep

To create a restorative yoga routine for better sleep, it's important to choose poses that promote relaxation and stress relief. Start by selecting a few key poses that target areas of tension in the body, such as the back, shoulders, and hips. You can then combine these poses into a sequence that flows smoothly and allows you to fully relax and release tension.

When practicing restorative yoga for better sleep, it's important to focus on your breath and stay present in the moment. By tuning into the sensations in your body and letting go of distractions, you can create a sense of calm and prepare for a restful night's sleep. It's also important to practice restorative yoga in a quiet and peaceful environment, free from distractions and noise.

Sweet Dreams: Restorative Yoga Poses for Deep, Restorative SleepSweet Dreams

In today's fast-paced world, it can be challenging to find time to relax and unwind before bed. Many of us struggle with falling asleep or staying asleep throughout the night, leading to feelings of fatigue and irritability the next day.

One way to combat this issue is through the practice of restorative yoga, a gentle and calming formof yoga that focuses on relaxation and deep breathing.

Restorative yoga poses are specifically designed to help the body and mind relax, release tension, and prepare fora restful night's sleep.

These poses are typically held for longer periods of time, allowing the body to fully relax and release any built-up stress or tension. By incorporating restorative yoga into your bedtime routine, you can create a sense of calm and peace that will help you drift off to sleep more easily and enjoy a more restorative night's rest.

One of the key benefits of restorative yoga is its ability to activate the parasympathetic nervous system, also known as the "rest and digest" system.

This system helps to calm the body and mind, reducing stress and promoting relaxation. By practicing restorative yoga before bed, you can signal to your body that it is time towind down and prepare for sleep, making it easier to fall asleep and stay asleep throughout the night.

To help you incorporate restorative yoga into your bedtime routine, we have compiled a list of restorative yoga poses that are perfect for promoting deep, restorative sleep.

These poses can be done in the comfort of your own home, with just a yoga mat and a few props such as blankets, bolsters, and pillows. By practicing these poses regularly, you can create a sense of calm and relaxation that will help you achieve a more restful night's sleep.

1. Supported Child's Pose (Balasana)

Start by kneeling on your mat with your big toes touching and your knees wide apart. Place a bolster or a stack of blankets in front of you and fold forward, resting your torso on the bolster or blankets. Extend your arms outin front of you or place them by your sides. Close your eyes and focus on your breath, allowing your body to relax and release any tension. Stay in this pose for 5-10 minutes, breathing deeply and allowing yourself to surrender to the support of the props.

2. Legs-Up-The-Wall Pose (Viparita Karani)

Sit with your right side against a wall and swing your legs up the wall as you lie back on your mat. You can place a bolster or a folded blanket under your hips for support. Extend your arms out to the sides with your palms facing up. Close your eyes and relax into the pose, focusing on your breath and allowing your body to release any tension. Stay in this pose for 5-10 minutes, breathing deeply and letting go of any stress or worries.

3. Reclining Bound Angle Pose (Supta Baddha Konasana)

Lie on your back with your knees bent and the soles of your feet together, allowing your knees to fall out to the sides. Place a bolster or a stack of blankets under your back for support.

You can also place pillows or blankets under your knees for added support. Close your eyes and relax into the pose, focusing on your breath and allowing your body to release any tension. Stay in this pose for 5-10 minutes, breathing deeply and surrendering to the support of the props.

4. Supported Bridge Pose (Setu Bandhasana)

Lie on your back with your knees bent and your feet hip-distance apart. Place a bolster or a stack of blankets under your hips and lift your hips up towards the sky.

You can also place a block or a pillow under your head for

support. Close your eyes and relax into the pose, focusing on your breath and allowing your body to release any tension. Stay in this pose for 5-10 minutes, breathing deeply and letting go of any stress or worries.

5. Corpse Pose (Savasana)

Lie on your back with your legs extended and your arms by your sides, palms facing up. Close your eyes and relax into the pose, allowing your body to fully surrender to the mat.

Focus on your breath, allowing it to become slow and steady. Stay in this pose for 10-15 minutes, breathing deeply and letting go of any thoughts or distractions. Allow yourself to drift off into a restful and rejuvenating sleep.

Incorporating restorative yoga poses into your bedtime routine can help you achieve a more restful and restorative night's sleep. By practicing these poses regularly, you can create a sense of calm and relaxation that will help you unwind before bed and prepare your body and mind for sleep.

Restorative Yoga: Your Ultimate Tool for a Restful Night

Restorative yoga is a gentle and relaxing form of yoga that focuses on deep relaxation and stress relief. It is theperfect tool for those looking to unwind and rejuvenate after a long day. Restorative yoga uses props such as blankets, bolsters, and blocks to support the body in various poses, allowing for a deep release of tension and asense of calm.

Many people struggle with stress and anxiety, especially at night when trying to wind down and get a restful night's sleep. Restorative yoga can be a powerful tool to help combat these feelings and promote a sense of peaceand relaxation.

By practicing restorative yoga before bed, you can create a soothing bedtime routine that will help you drift off to sleep more easily and wake up feeling refreshed and rejuvenated.

One of the key benefits of restorative yoga is its ability to activate the parasympathetic nervous system, also known as the "rest and digest" system.

This system is responsible for promoting relaxation, reducing stress, and lowering blood pressure. By practicing restorative yoga, you can help activate this system and trigger the body's natural relaxation response, leading to a deep sense of calm and tranquility.

Restorative yoga is also beneficial for those who struggle with insomnia or other sleep disorders. By practicing restorative yoga before bed, you can help calm the mind and body, making it easier to fall asleep and stay asleepthroughout the night.

The gentle, supportive poses of restorative yoga can help release tension and promote a sense of relaxation, making it an ideal practice for those looking to improve their sleep quality.

In addition to its physical benefits, restorative yoga also has numerous mental and emotional benefits. The practice of restorative yoga encourages mindfulness and self-awareness, helping you to connect with your body and quiet the mind. By focusing on your breath and being present in the moment, you can cultivate a sense of inner peace and serenity that can carry over into your daily life.

Restorative yoga can also be a powerful tool for managing stress and anxiety. By practicing restorative yoga regularly, you can learn to release tension and let go of negative thoughts and emotions.

The deep relaxation and gentle stretching of restorative yoga can help calm the nervous system and promote a sense of balance and well-being.

This can be especially beneficial for those who struggle with chronic stress or anxiety, as restorative yoga offers a safe and nurturing space to unwind and recharge.

If you're new to restorative yoga, it's important to start slowly and listen to your body. Begin with simple poses and gradually work your way up to more advanced poses as you become more comfortable with the practice. Remember to use props to support your body in each pose, and focus on deep, mindful breathing to help relax the mind and body.

To get started with restorative yoga, try incorporating a few simple poses into your bedtime routine. Start by setting up a quiet, comfortable space with a yoga mat and any props you may need, such as blankets, bolsters, or blocks. Begin by sitting in a comfortable position and taking a few deep breaths to center yourself.

Next, try the following restorative yoga poses to help you relax and unwind before bed:

1. Supported Child's Pose: Begin by kneeling on the mat with your big toes touching and knees slightly apart. Place a bolster or folded blanket between your knees and lower your torso onto the prop, resting your forehead on the mat. Extend your arms out in front of you or place them by your sides. Close your eyes and focus on your

breath, allowing your body to relax and release tension.

2.   Legs-Up-the-Wall Pose: Sit with your right side against a wall and swing your legs up the wall as you lie backon the mat. Place a bolster or folded blanket under your hips for support. Extend your arms out to the sides or place them on your belly. Close your eyes and relax into the pose, focusing on your breath and allowing your body to release tension.

3.   Supported Reclining Twist: Lie on your back with your knees bent and feet flat on the mat. Shift your hipsslightly to the right and extend your arms out to the sides in a T position. Inhale and exhale as you lower your knees to the left, resting them on a bolster or folded blanket. Turn your head to the right and close your eyes, focusing on your breath and allowing your body to release tension.

4. Supported Savasana: Lie on your back with your legs extended and arms by your sides. Place a bolster or folded blanket under your knees for support. Close your eyes and focus on your breath, allowing your body to relax completely. Stay in this pose for several minutes, letting go of any tension or stress.

By incorporating these restorative yoga poses into your bedtime routine, you can create a calming and soothing practice that will help you relax and unwind before sleep.

Chapter 8: The Zen of Sleep: Restorative Yoga Practices for Better Rest The Zen of Sleep

In today's fast-paced world, many people struggle to get a good night's sleep. The stresses and demands of daily life can leave us feeling tired and restless, making it difficult to relax and unwind at the end of the day. However, there is a solution that can help you achieve better rest and relaxation: restorative yoga.

Restorative yoga is a gentle and soothing form of yoga that focuses on relaxation and rejuvenation. It involves holding gentle poses for an extended period of time, allowing the body to fully relax and release tension. By practicing restorative yoga before bed, you can calm your mind, reduce stress, and prepare your body for a restful night's sleep.

One of the key principles of restorative yoga is the concept of mindfulness. Mindfulness involves being fully present in the moment and paying attention to your thoughts, feelings, and sensations without judgment.

By practicing mindfulness during restorative yoga, you can quiet your mind and create a sense of inner peace that will help you drift off to sleep more easily.

Another important aspect of restorative yoga is the use of props. Props such as blankets, bolsters, and blocks can help support your body in various poses, allowing you to relax more deeply and comfortably. By using props, youcan release tension in your muscles, improve your posture, and enhance your overall sense of well-being.

In addition to promoting relaxation, restorative yoga can also help improve your flexibility and range of motion. By gently stretching and lengthening your muscles in restorative poses, you can increase blood flow to your muscles and joints, reduce stiffness and soreness, and improve your overall physical health.

To get started with restorative yoga, it's important to create a peaceful and comfortable environment for your practice. Choose a quiet, dimly lit space where you won't be disturbed, and gather any props you may need foryour practice. You may also want to play soft music or use aromatherapy oils to enhance the relaxing atmosphere.

Once you're ready to begin, start by focusing on your breath. Take slow, deep breaths in and out through yournose, allowing your breath to become slow and steady. As you breathe, bring your awareness to your body andnotice any areas of tension or discomfort.

Next, begin to move into restorative poses. Some common restorative poses include Child's Pose, Legs-Up-the-Wall Pose, and Supported Bridge Pose. Hold each pose for several minutes, focusing on relaxing your body andmind with each breath.

As you practice restorative yoga, remember to listen to your body and make any adjustments that feel comfortable and supportive. If a pose feels too intense or uncomfortable, back off and try a gentler variation.The goal of restorative yoga is not to push yourself to the limit, but to create a sense of ease and relaxation inyour body and mind.

After completing your restorative yoga practice, take a few moments to lie down in Savasana, or Corpse Pose. Allow your body to fully relax and surrender to the floor, letting go of any remaining tension or stress. Stay in Savasana for at least 5-10 minutes, focusing on your breath and allowing your mind to become still and quiet.

By incorporating restorative yoga into your bedtime routine, you can create a sense of calm and relaxation that will help you fall asleep more easily and enjoy a more restful night's sleep. With regular practice, you may find that your sleep improves, your energy levels increase, and your overall sense of well-being improves.

In addition to practicing restorative yoga, there are several other tips you can try to improve your sleep quality. These include:

- Establishing a consistent bedtime routine: Going to bed and waking up at the same time each day can help regulate your body's internal clock and improve your sleep quality.

- Creating a comfortable sleep environment: Make sure your bedroom is dark, quiet, and at a comfortable temperature for sleeping. Invest in a comfortable mattress and pillows to support your body while you sleep.

- Limiting screen time before bed: The blue light emitted by electronic devices can interfere with your body's natural sleep-wake cycle. Try to avoid screens at least an hour before bed to help your body relax and prepare forsleep.

- Avoiding caffeine and heavy meals before bed: Consuming caffeine or large meals close to bedtime can disruptyour sleep and make it harder to relax. Try to avoid these substances in the hours leading up to bedtime.

- Practicing relaxation techniques: In addition to restorative yoga, you can try other relaxation techniques such as deep breathing, meditation, or progressive muscle relaxation to help calm your mind and body before bed.

By incorporating these tips and practices into your nightly routine, you can create a sense of peace and tranquility that will help you achieve better rest and relaxation.

Restorative Yoga: Your Gateway to a Good Night's Sleep

Restorative yoga is a gentle form of yoga that focuses on relaxation and rejuvenation. It is a perfect practice for those who are looking to unwind and de-stress after a long day.

Restorative yoga can be particularly beneficial for those who struggle with sleep issues, as it helps to calm the mind and relax the body, making it easier to fall asleep and stay asleep throughout the night.

In today's fast-paced world, many of us struggle to get a good night's sleep. Whether it's due to stress, anxiety, or simply an inability to relax, sleep deprivation can have a serious impact on our overall health and well-being.

Restorative yoga offers a natural and effective way to combat sleep issues, allowing you to achieve a deep and restful night's sleep without the use of medication.

So how exactly does restorative yoga help to improve sleep? Restorative yoga involves a series of gentle poses that are held for an extended period of time, typically between five to 20 minutes.

These poses are designed to release tension in the body, calm the mind, and promote relaxation. By focusing on deep breathing and mindfulness, restorative yoga helps to activate the body's parasympathetic nervous system, also known as the "rest and digest" system. This triggers the body's relaxation response, reducing stress hormones and promoting a sense of calm and well-being.

One of the key benefits of restorative yoga is its ability to quiet the mind and reduce mental chatter.

Many of us struggle to fall asleep because our minds are racing with thoughts and worries. Restorative yoga encourages us to focus on the present moment, letting go of stress and anxiety and allowing ourselves to fully relax.

By practicing restorative yoga before bed, you can create a peaceful and tranquil environment that is conducive to sleep.

Another benefit of restorative yoga is its ability to release physical tension in the body. Many of us carry stress and tension in our muscles, which can lead to discomfort and pain, making it difficult to relax and fall asleep.

The gentle stretches and poses of restorative yoga help to release this tension, promoting a sense of ease and comfort in the body. By releasing physical tension, you can create a more comfortable and restful environment for sleep.

In addition to promoting relaxation and reducing tension,

restorative yoga can also help to improve overall sleep quality. By calming the mind and relaxing the body, restorative yoga can help you to fall asleep more quickly and stay asleep throughout the night.

The deep breathing and mindfulness practices of restorative yoga can also help to improve the quality of your sleep, allowing you to wake up feeling refreshed and rejuvenated.

So how can you incorporate restorative yoga into your bedtime routine? Here are some tips to help you get started:

1. Create a peaceful environment: Find a quiet and comfortable space where you can practice restorative yoga without distractions. Dim the lights, play soft music, and light a candle or incense to create a calming atmosphere.

2. Choose gentle poses: Select a few restorative yoga poses that focus on relaxation and release tension in the body. Some popular poses include Child's Pose, Legs Up the Wall, and Corpse Pose. Hold each pose for several minutes, focusing on deep breathing and relaxation.

3. Practice deep breathing: Incorporate deep breathing exercises into your restorative yoga practice to help calm the mind and relax the body. Focus on breathing deeply into the belly, inhaling and exhaling slowly and evenly.

4. Set aside time for relaxation: Make time for restorative yoga

in your bedtime routine, ideally at least 15-20 minutes before you plan to go to sleep. This will allow you to unwind and prepare your body and mind for arestful night's sleep.

5. Listen to your body: Pay attention to how your body feels during your restorative yoga practice. If a pose feels uncomfortable or painful, gently come out of it and try a different pose. Listen to your body's cues and adjust your practice accordingly.

Incorporating restorative yoga into your bedtime routine can have a profound impact on your sleep quality and overall well-being. By practicing gentle poses, deep breathing, and mindfulness, you can create a peaceful and tranquil environment that is conducive to sleep. Give restorative yoga a try and experience the benefits of a goodnight's sleep.

Sleep Tight with Restorative Yoga: A Complete Guide

Sleep is essential for overall health and well-being. It allows our bodies to rest, repair, and recharge, ensuring that we have the energy and focus we need to tackle the challenges of each day.

Unfortunately, many people struggle with getting a good night's sleep, whether it's due to stress, anxiety, or simply an inability to relax and unwind.

Restorative yoga is a gentle and soothing form of yoga that focuses on relaxation and stress relief. By incorporating restorative yoga into your bedtime routine, you can help calm your mind, release tension in your body, and prepare yourself for a restful night's sleep.

 In this guide, we will explore the benefits of restorative yoga for sleep, as well as provide you with a step-by-step plan for incorporating it into your nightly routine.

Benefits of Restorative Yoga for Sleep

Restorative yoga is a practice that involves holding gentle, supported poses for extended periods of time. This allows the body to relax deeply, releasing tension and stress from the muscles and calming the mind. By practicing restorative yoga before bed, you can help prepare your body and mind for sleep in the following ways:

1. Stress Relief: Restorative yoga helps to activate the parasympathetic nervous system, which is responsible for the body's "rest and digest" response. This can help reduce levels of the stress hormone cortisol, allowing you to relax and unwind before bed.

2. Muscle Relaxation: By holding gentle poses for an extended period of time, restorative yoga helps to release tension and tightness in the muscles. This can help alleviate physical discomfort and promote a sense of ease and relaxation in the body.

3. Mindfulness: Restorative yoga encourages you to focus on your breath and be present in the moment. This can help quiet the mind and reduce racing thoughts, making it easier to let go of the day's stressors and prepare for sleep.

4. Improved Sleep Quality: By promoting relaxation and stress relief, restorative yoga can help improve the quality of your sleep. You may find that you fall asleep more easily, stay asleep longer, and wake up feeling more refreshed and rejuvenated.

How to Incorporate Restorative Yoga into Your Bedtime Routine

Now that you understand the benefits of restorative yoga for sleep, let's explore how you can incorporate this practice into your bedtime routine. Follow these steps to create a restorative yoga routine that will help you relaxand unwind before bed:

1. Set the Scene: Create a calm and peaceful environment for your restorative yoga practice. Dim the lights, light a candle or some incense, and play soft, soothing music to help set the mood for relaxation.

2. Gather Your Props: You will need some props to support you in your restorative yoga poses. This may include a yoga mat, bolsters, blankets, pillows, and blocks. Make sure you have everything you need within reach before you begin your practice.

3. Start with Gentle Movement: Begin your restorative yoga practice with some gentle movement to help warm
up the body and prepare it for relaxation. This may include some seated stretches, gentle twists, or a few rounds of Cat-Cow pose.

4. Practice Supported Poses: Choose a few restorative yoga poses that you find particularly relaxing and soothing. Some common restorative poses include Supported Child's Pose, Legs-Up-the-Wall Pose, and Reclining Bound Angle Pose. Use your props to support yourself in these poses and hold them for 5-10 minuteseach.

5. Focus on Your Breath: As you hold each restorative pose, focus on your breath and try to cultivate a sense of deep relaxation. Take slow, deep breaths in and out through your

nose, allowing each exhale to release tension and stress from your body.

6.   Relax and Let Go: Allow yourself to fully relax and let go of any tension or stress as you hold each restorative pose. Surrender to the support of your props and the earth beneath you, allowing yourself to sink deeper into a state of relaxation with each breath.

7.   End with Savasana: Finish your restorative yoga practice with a few minutes of Savasana, or Corpse Pose. Lieflat on your back with your arms and legs extended, allowing your body to completely relax and surrender to the earth. Stay here for at least 5-10 minutes, focusing on your breath and allowing yourself to fully let go.

8.   Prepare for Sleep: After you finish your restorative yoga practice, take a few moments to prepare yourself forsleep. Dim the lights further, turn off any screens or electronic devices, and make sure your bedroom is cool, dark, and quiet. Slip into comfortable pajamas and climb into bed, ready to drift off into a restful night's sleep.

Chapter 9: Restorative Yoga: The Key to Unlocking Better Sleep

In today's fast-paced world, many of us struggle to get a good night's sleep. Whether it's due to stress, anxiety, or just the general busyness of life, sleep can often feel elusive. However, there is a powerful tool that can help you achieve the restful sleep you deserve: restorative yoga.

Restorative yoga is a gentle and soothing form of yoga that focuses on relaxation and deep rest. It involves holding poses for an extended period of time, typically 5-20 minutes, while using props such as blankets, bolsters, and blocks to support the body.

This allows the muscles to fully relax and the mind to quieten, leadingto a state of deep relaxation and rejuvenation.

One of the key benefits of restorative yoga is its ability to activate the parasympathetic nervous system, also known as the "rest and digest" system.

This system is responsible for promoting relaxation, slowing the heart rate, and calming the mind. By engaging the parasympathetic nervous system through restorative yoga, you caneffectively reduce stress and anxiety, making it easier to fall asleep and stay asleep throughout the night.

Another benefit of restorative yoga is its ability to release tension and tightness in the body. Many of us carry stress and tension in our muscles, which can lead to discomfort and pain, especially when trying to sleep.

By practicing restorative yoga, you can gently stretch and release these tight areas, allowing the body to relax and unwind. This can help alleviate physical discomfort and promote a sense of ease and comfort, making it easier to drift off to sleep.

In addition to its physical benefits, restorative yoga also offers mental and emotional benefits that can improve sleep quality. By focusing on deep breathing and mindfulness during restorative yoga practice, you can quiet the mind and release racing thoughts, helping to calm the nervous system and promote a sense of peace and tranquility.

This can be particularly helpful for those who struggle with insomnia or other sleep disorders, as it can help quiet the mind and prepare the body for restful sleep.

So how exactly can you incorporate restorative yoga into your bedtime routine to unlock better sleep? Here are some tips to help you get started:

1. Create a calming environment: Set the mood for relaxation

by dimming the lights, lighting candles, and playing soft music. Create a cozy space with blankets, pillows, and props to support your body during restorativeyoga poses.

2. Choose a few restorative poses: There are many restorative yoga poses to choose from, but some of the mostbeneficial for sleep include legs up the wall pose, supported child's pose, reclining bound angle pose, and supported savasana. Hold each pose for 5-10 minutes, focusing on deep breathing and relaxation.

3. Practice deep breathing: Deep breathing is a key component of restorative yoga, as it helps to calm the mindand relax the body. Focus on slow, deep breaths throughout your practice, inhaling and exhaling through the nose.

4. Release tension: As you hold each restorative pose, focus on releasing tension and tightness in the body. Relaxyour muscles, soften your breath, and allow yourself to sink deeper into the pose with each exhale.

5. Stay present: Mindfulness is an important aspect of restorative yoga, so try to stay present and focused on the sensations in your body as you practice. Notice any areas of tension or discomfort, and gently release them with each breath.

6. Wind down before bed: After your restorative yoga

practice, take some time to wind down before bed. Avoid screens, caffeine, and stimulating activities, and instead opt for a warm bath, reading a book, or practicing gentle stretches to further relax the body and mind.

By incorporating restorative yoga into your bedtime routine, you can unlock better sleep and wake up feeling refreshed and rejuvenated. So why not give it a try tonight and see the difference it can make in your sleep quality? Restorative yoga may just be the key to unlocking the restful sleep you've been longing for.

Deep Sleep, Deep Relaxation: Restorative Yoga Practices

Deep sleep is essential for our overall well-being and health. It is during deep sleep that our bodies repair and rejuvenate themselves, allowing us to wake up feeling refreshed and energized. However, many of us struggle to achieve deep sleep due to various factors such as stress, anxiety, and poor sleep habits.

One effective way to promote deep sleep and relaxation is through restorative yoga practices. Restorative yoga is a gentle and therapeutic form of yoga that focuses on relaxation and rejuvenation.

By incorporating restorative yoga into your bedtime routine, you can help calm your mind, release tension in your body, and prepare yourself for a restful night's sleep.

There are several restorative yoga poses that are particularly beneficial for promoting deep sleep and relaxation. These poses help to activate the parasympathetic nervous system, which is responsible for the body's rest and relaxation response. By activating this system, you can help reduce stress and anxiety, lower your heart rate, and promote feelings of calm and tranquility.

One of the most popular restorative yoga poses for deep sleep is Legs-Up-The-Wall pose. To practice this pose, simply lie on your back with your legs extended up against a wall. This pose helps to improve circulation, reduce swelling in the legs, and calm the nervous system. By practicing Legs-Up-The-Wall pose before bed, you can help relax your body and mind, making it easier to fall asleep and stay asleep throughout the night.

Another restorative yoga pose that is beneficial for deep sleep is Child's pose. To practice this pose, kneel on the floor with your big toes touching and your knees spread apart.

Slowly lower your torso down to rest on your thighs, extending your arms out in front of you. Child's pose helps to release tension in the back, shoulders, and neck, allowing you to relax and unwind before bedtime.

In addition to specific restorative yoga poses, incorporating deep breathing exercises into your bedtime routine can also help promote deep sleep and relaxation. Deep breathing helps to calm the mind, reduce stress, and promote feelings of relaxation.

One effective deep breathing exercise to try before bed is the 4-7-8 breathing technique. To practice this technique, inhale for a count of 4, hold your breath for a count of 7, and exhale for a count of 8. Repeat this cycle several times to help calm your mind and prepare yourself for deep sleep.

In addition to restorative yoga poses and deep breathing exercises, creating a restful sleep environment can also help promote deep sleep and relaxation. Make sure your bedroom is dark, quiet, and cool, and avoid using electronic devices before bed. Establishing a bedtime routine that includes restorative yoga practices, deep breathing exercises, and a calming sleep environment can help you achieve deep sleep and wake up feeling refreshed and rejuvenated.

Overall, restorative yoga practices are a powerful tool for promoting deep sleep and relaxation. By incorporating restorative yoga poses, deep breathing exercises, and creating a restful sleep environment into your bedtime routine, you can help calm your mind, release tension in your body, and prepare yourself for a restful night's sleep.

Prioritizing deep sleep is essential for our overall health and well-being, so why not give restorative yoga a try and see the benefits for yourself?

Restorative Yoga: Your Solution for Sleepless Nights

In today's fast-paced world, many people struggle with sleepless nights. Whether it's due to stress, anxiety, orsimply an inability to relax, the consequences of not getting enough sleep can be severe.

From decreased cognitive function to increased risk of chronic diseases, the importance of a good night's sleep cannot be overstated.

One solution that has been gaining popularity in recent years is restorative yoga. This gentle form of yoga focuses on relaxation and stress relief, making it an ideal practice for those who struggle with sleep issues.

 In thisarticle, we'll explore the benefits of restorative yoga for sleep, as well as provide some tips on how to incorporateit into your nightly routine.

What is Restorative Yoga?

Restorative yoga is a form of yoga that focuses on relaxation and rejuvenation. Unlike more vigorous forms ofyoga, such as vinyasa or power yoga, restorative yoga involves holding gentle poses for an extended period of time. These poses are designed to release tension in the body and promote a sense of calm and relaxation.

Restorative yoga often incorporates props such as bolsters, blankets, and blocks to support the body in each pose. By providing support and allowing the body to fully relax, these props help to deepen the benefits of each pose and promote a sense of deep relaxation.

Benefits of Restorative Yoga for Sleep

There are many benefits to incorporating restorative yoga into your nightly routine, especially if you struggle with sleepless nights. Some of the key benefits of restorative yoga for sleep include:

1. Stress Relief: One of the primary benefits of restorative yoga is its ability to reduce stress and promote relaxation. By focusing on deep breathing and gentle movement, restorative yoga helps to calm the nervous system and release tension in the body. This can help to reduce feelings of anxiety and promote a sense of calmbefore bedtime.

2. Improved Sleep Quality: Restorative yoga can also help to improve the quality of your sleep. By promoting relaxation and reducing stress, restorative yoga can help you fall asleep more easily and stay asleep throughoutthe night. This can lead to a more restful and rejuvenating night's sleep, allowing you to wake up feeling refreshed and energized.

3. Muscle Relaxation: Many people carry tension in their muscles, especially in areas such as the neck, shoulders, and back. Restorative yoga can help to release this tension and promote relaxation in the muscles, making it easier to unwind and prepare for sleep.

4. Mind-Body Connection: Restorative yoga also helps to cultivate a strong mind-body connection, which can be beneficial for those who struggle with sleep issues. By focusing on the breath and being present in the moment, restorative yoga can help to quiet the mind and promote a sense of inner peace.

Tips for Incorporating Restorative Yoga into Your Nightly Routine

If you're interested in trying restorative yoga to help with your sleep issues, here are some tips to help you incorporate it into your nightly routine:

1. Create a Relaxing Environment: To fully benefit from restorative yoga, it's important to create a relaxing environment in which to practice. Choose a quiet, dimly lit space and gather any props you may need, such as bolsters, blankets, and blocks. You may also want to play soft music or light candles to enhance the calming atmosphere.

2. Practice Before Bedtime: Aim to practice restorative yoga before bedtime to help prepare your body andmind for sleep. A short 15-20 minute practice can be enough to reap the benefits of restorative yoga and promote relaxation before bedtime.

3. Focus on Deep Breathing: Throughout your restorative yoga practice, focus on deep, slow breathing to help calm the nervous system and promote relaxation. Take long, slow breaths in and out through the nose, allowing the breath to deepen and the body to relax with each exhale.

4. Listen to Your Body: As you move through each restorative yoga pose, listen to your body and adjust asneeded. If a pose feels uncomfortable or causes pain, come out of it and find a more comfortable position. Remember, restorative yoga is about relaxation, so it's important to honor your body's needs and limitations.

5. End with Savasana: Finish your restorative yoga practice with a few minutes of savasana, or corpse pose. Lieflat on your back with your arms and legs extended, allowing your body to fully relax and sink into the floor. Focus on your breath and allow any remaining tension to melt away, preparing your body and mind for a restfulnight's sleep.

In conclusion, restorative yoga can be a powerful tool for promoting relaxation and improving sleep quality. By incorporating restorative yoga into your nightly routine, you can reduce stress, release tension in the body, and cultivate a sense of calm and inner peace before bedtime.

Chapter 10: Restorative Yoga for Better Sleep: Tips and Techniques for Relaxation

Restorative yoga is a gentle form of yoga that focuses on relaxation and stress relief. It involves using props such as blankets, bolsters, and blocks to support the body in various poses, allowing for deep relaxation and rejuvenation. Restorative yoga is particularly beneficial for those struggling with sleep issues, as it helps to calm the mind and body, promoting a sense of peace and tranquility that can lead to better sleep.

In today's fast-paced world, many people struggle to get a good night's sleep. Stress, anxiety, and a busy schedule can all contribute to sleepless nights and restless sleep. Restorative yoga offers a natural and effective way to combat these issues and improve the quality of your sleep.

 By practicing restorative yoga regularly, you can create a bedtime routine that promotes relaxation and prepares your body and mind for a restful night's sleep.

Here are some tips and techniques for incorporating restorative yoga into your bedtime routine to help you getbetter sleep:

1. Create a Relaxing Environment: Before you begin your

restorative yoga practice, create a peaceful and calming environment in your bedroom. Dim the lights, play soft music, and light a candle or use essential oils to create a soothing atmosphere that will help you relax and unwind.

2. Practice Deep Breathing: Deep breathing is a key component of restorative yoga and can help to calm the mind and body. Before you begin your yoga practice, take a few moments to focus on your breath. Inhale deeply through your nose, filling your lungs with air, and exhale slowly through your mouth, releasing any tension or stress.

3. Use Props: Props are essential for a restorative yoga practice, as they help to support the body in various poses and promote deep relaxation. Use blankets, bolsters, pillows, and blocks to create a comfortable and supportive environment for your practice.

4. Focus on Gentle Poses: Restorative yoga poses are gentle and passive, allowing the body to relax fully. Focus on poses that open the chest, lengthen the spine, and release tension in the hips and shoulders.

Some popular restorative yoga poses for better sleep include Legs-Up-The-Wall pose, Supported Child's pose, and Reclining Bound Angle pose.

5. Hold Poses for Several Minutes: In restorative yoga, poses are typically held for several minutes to allow the body to fully

relax and release tension. As you hold each pose, focus on your breath and allow yourself to sink deeper into relaxation with each exhale.

6. Practice Yoga Nidra: Yoga Nidra, or yogic sleep, is a guided meditation practice that promotes deep relaxation and restful sleep. You can find guided Yoga Nidra meditations online or through yoga apps, or you can create your own practice by focusing on relaxation techniques and visualization.

7. End with Savasana: Savasana, or Corpse pose, is the final relaxation pose in a yoga practice and is essential forcalming the mind and body before sleep. Lie on your back with your arms and legs extended, close your eyes, and focus on your breath as you relax fully into the pose.

8. Establish a Bedtime Routine: Incorporate restorative yoga into your bedtime routine to signal to your body that it's time to relax and prepare for sleep. Practice gentle yoga poses, deep breathing, and relaxation techniques
before bed to help you unwind and let go of the stresses of the day.

9. Listen to Your Body: Pay attention to how your body feels during your restorative yoga practice and adjustyour poses and props as needed. If a pose feels uncomfortable or causes pain, come out of it slowly and find a more comfortable position. Remember, restorative yoga is about relaxation and comfort, so

listen to your bodyand honor its needs.

10. Be Consistent: Consistency is key when it comes to incorporating restorative yoga into your bedtime routine.Make an effort to practice restorative yoga regularly, whether it's every night before bed or a few times a week.Over time, you'll notice the benefits of better sleep and improved relaxation from your practice.

In conclusion, restorative yoga is a powerful tool for promoting better sleep and relaxation. By incorporating restorative yoga into your bedtime routine and practicing gentle poses, deep breathing, and relaxation techniques,you can create a peaceful and calming environment that prepares your body and mind for a restful night's sleep.

Remember to listen to your body, be consistent with your practice, and enjoy the benefits of improved sleep and overall well-being. Restorative yoga for better sleep is a natural and effective way to combat sleep issues and promote a sense of peace and tranquility in your life.

Restorative Yoga: The Ultimate Sleep Aid

Restorative yoga is a gentle form of yoga that focuses on relaxation and deep rest. It is the ultimate sleep aid for those who struggle with insomnia, stress, or anxiety. Restorative yoga uses props such as blankets, bolsters, and blocks to support the body in various poses, allowing the muscles to relax and the mind to calm.

Restorative yoga is different from other forms of yoga in that it is not about stretching or strengthening the body. Instead, it is about finding stillness and quieting the mind. This makes it the perfect practice for those who have trouble falling asleep or staying asleep.

The benefits of restorative yoga for sleep are numerous. One of the main benefits is that it helps to reduce stress and anxiety, which are common causes of sleep problems. By focusing on deep breathing and relaxation, restorative yoga can help to calm the nervous system and promote a sense of peace and well-being.

Another benefit of restorative yoga for sleep is that it can help to improve circulation and digestion. By gently stretching and opening the body, restorative yoga can help to release tension and promote better blood flow. This can help to relax the body and prepare it for sleep.

Restorative yoga can also help to improve flexibility and range of motion. By holding gentle poses for an extended period of time, restorative yoga can help to release tight muscles and improve joint mobility. This can help to reduce pain and stiffness, making it easier to relax and fall asleep.

One of the key benefits of restorative yoga for sleep is that it can help to quiet the mind. By focusing on the breath and the sensations in the body, restorative yoga can help to quiet the mental chatter that can keep us awake at night. This can help to promote a sense of calm and relaxation, making it easier to drift off to sleep.

There are many restorative yoga poses that are particularly beneficial for sleep. One of the most popular poses issupported child's pose, where the body is supported by bolsters and blankets in a gentle forward fold. This posecan help to release tension in the back and shoulders, making it easier to relax and fall asleep.

Another restorative yoga pose that is great for sleep is legs up the wall pose. In this pose, the legs are elevated against a wall while the body rests on the floor. This pose can help to improve circulation and reduce swelling in the legs, making it easier to relax and fall asleep.

Corpse pose is another restorative yoga pose that is perfect for sleep. In this pose, the body lies flat on the back with the arms and legs extended. This pose can help to release tension in the entire body and promote deep relaxation, making it easier to fall asleep.

To get the most benefit from restorative yoga for sleep, it is important to create a calming and peaceful environment. This may include dimming the lights, playing soft music, and using aromatherapy oils such as lavender or chamomile. It is also important to practice restorative yoga in a quiet and comfortable space where you will not be disturbed.

It is recommended to practice restorative yoga for sleep in the evening, before bedtime. This can help to calm the mind and prepare the body for sleep. A restorative yoga practice for sleep may last anywhere from 15 minutes to an hour, depending on your preference and schedule.

In addition to practicing restorative yoga for sleep, there are other lifestyle changes that can help to improve sleep. This may include creating a bedtime routine, avoiding caffeine and electronic devices before bed, and creating a comfortable sleep environment.

By incorporating restorative yoga into your bedtime routine, you can help to promote deep relaxation and improve the quality of your sleep.

In conclusion, restorative yoga is the ultimate sleep aid for those who struggle with insomnia, stress, or anxiety.By focusing on relaxation and deep rest, restorative yoga can help to calm the mind, release tension in the body, and promote a sense of peace and well-being.

By incorporating restorative yoga into your bedtime routine, you can help to improve the quality of your sleep and wake up feeling refreshed and rejuvenated. So, why not give restorative yoga a try and experience the benefits for yourself?

Restorative Yoga: Your Prescription for Better Sleep

Restorative yoga is a gentle form of yoga that focuses on relaxation and rejuvenation. It is a practice that is perfect for those looking to improve their sleep quality and overall well-being.

In this article, we will explore the benefits of restorative yoga for better sleep and how you can incorporate it into your daily routine.

Restorative yoga is a form of yoga that is focused on relaxation and restoration. It involves using props such as bolsters, blankets, and blocks to support the body in various poses.

The practice is slow-paced and gentle, allowing the body to relax deeply and release tension. Restorative yoga is perfect for those who are looking to unwind and de-stress after a long day.

One of the main benefits of restorative yoga is its ability to help improve sleep quality. Many people struggle with sleep issues, whether it be difficulty falling asleep, staying asleep, or waking up feeling tired and unrested. Restorative yoga can help address these issues by calming the mind and body, reducing stress and anxiety, and promoting relaxation.

Restorative yoga helps activate the parasympathetic nervous

system, also known as the "rest and digest" system. This system is responsible for slowing down the heart rate, relaxing the muscles, and promoting a state of calm and relaxation. By practicing restorative yoga, you can help trigger the parasympathetic nervous system, allowing your body to relax and prepare for sleep.

In addition to promoting relaxation, restorative yoga can also help reduce stress and anxiety. Many people struggle with stress and anxiety, which can have a negative impact on sleep quality.

Restorative yoga helps calm the mind and body, allowing you to release tension and worries. By practicing restorative yoga regularly, you can help reduce stress and anxiety levels, leading to better sleep quality.

Another benefit of restorative yoga is its ability to help improve flexibility and mobility. Many people experience tightness and stiffness in their muscles, which can make it difficult to relax and fall asleep. Restorative yoga helps stretch and release tension in the muscles, allowing for greater flexibility and mobility. By practicing restorative yoga, you can help improve your overall physical well-being, leading to better sleep quality.

So, how can you incorporate restorative yoga into your daily routine to help improve your sleep quality? Here are some tips to get you started:

1. Set aside time each day for restorative yoga practice. Find a quiet and comfortable space where you can practice without distractions. Aim to practice for at least 15-20 minutes each day to experience the full benefitsof restorative yoga.

2. Gather your props. You will need a bolster, blanket, and blocks to support your body in various poses. These props will help you relax deeply and release tension in the body. If you don't have props, you can use pillows andtowels as alternatives.

3. Start with simple poses. Begin your restorative yoga practice with simple poses such as Child's Pose, Legs-Up-The-Wall Pose, and Supported Bridge Pose. These poses will help you relax and unwind, preparing your body for sleep.

4. Focus on your breath. Pay attention to your breath as you move through each pose. Take slow, deep breaths tohelp calm the mind and body. By focusing on your breath, you can help reduce stress and anxiety, leading to better sleep quality.

5. Listen to your body. As you practice restorative yoga, listen to your body and adjust the poses as needed. If a pose feels uncomfortable or painful, come out of it and try a different variation. It's important to honor your body and practice with compassion and self-care.

6. End with relaxation. After you have completed your restorative yoga practice, end with a relaxation pose such as Savasana. Lie on your back with your arms and legs extended, allowing your body to completely relax and unwind. Stay in this pose for a few minutes, focusing on your breath and letting go of any tension or stress.

By incorporating restorative yoga into your daily routine, you can help improve your sleep quality and overall well-being. This gentle practice can help calm the mind and body, reduce stress and anxiety, and promote relaxation.

Whether you are struggling with sleep issues or simply looking to unwind and de-stress, restorative yoga can be a powerful tool to help you achieve better sleep.

In conclusion, restorative yoga is a gentle and effective practice for improving sleep quality. By incorporating restorative yoga into your daily routine, you can help calm the mind and body, reduce stress and anxiety, and promote relaxation.

Whether you are a beginner or an experienced yogi, restorative yoga can be a valuable tool for achieving better sleep and overall well-being. So, roll out your mat, grab your props, and start practicing restorative yoga today for a restful night's sleep.

Chapter 11: The Sleep Solution: Restorative Yoga Practices for Deep Rest

The Sleep Solution: Restorative Yoga Practices for Deep Rest is a comprehensive guide to using restorative yoga to improve the quality of your sleep.

 This book offers a variety of yoga poses and techniques that can help you relax your body and mind, promoting deep rest and rejuvenation.

In today's fast-paced world, many people struggle with getting enough quality sleep. Stress, anxiety, and busy schedules can all contribute to poor sleep patterns, leading to fatigue, irritability, and a host of other health issues.

However, by incorporating restorative yoga into your bedtime routine, you can create a peaceful and calming environment that promotes deep rest and relaxation.

Restorative yoga is a gentle and therapeutic form of yoga that focuses on relaxation and stress relief. Unlike more vigorous styles of yoga, restorative yoga poses are held for an extended period of time, allowing the body to fully relax and release tension. By practicing restorative yoga before bed, you can calm your nervous system, quiet your mind, and prepare your body for a restful night's sleep.

The Sleep Solution: Restorative Yoga Practices for Deep Rest provides a step-by-step guide to incorporating restorative yoga into your nightly routine.

The book begins by explaining the science behind sleep and the importance of deep rest for overall health and well-being. It then introduces the concept of restorative yoga and how it can help improve the quality of your sleep.

The book includes a variety of restorative yoga poses that are specifically designed to promote relaxation and deep rest. Each pose is accompanied by detailed instructions and illustrations, making it easy for readers to follow along and practice the poses at home. The poses range from gentle stretches to supported inversions, allowing you to customize your practice based on your individual needs and preferences.

In addition to the yoga poses, The Sleep Solution also includes breathing techniques, meditation practices, and mindfulness exercises that can enhance the restorative effects of your yoga practice. By combining these techniques with the restorative yoga poses, you can create a comprehensive bedtime routine that promotes deep relaxation and restful sleep.

One of the key benefits of restorative yoga is its ability to activate the parasympathetic nervous system, also known as the "rest and digest" system. This system is responsible for promoting relaxation, reducing stress, and preparing the body for sleep. By practicing restorative yoga before bed, you can stimulate the parasympathetic nervous system and create a sense of calm and tranquility that can help you fall asleep more easily and stay asleep throughout the night.

Another benefit of restorative yoga is its ability to release tension and tightness in the body. Many people hold stress and tension in their muscles, leading to stiffness, discomfort, and pain. By practicing restorative yoga poses that target specific areas of tension, you can release tightness, improve flexibility, and create a sense of ease and comfort in your body.

The Sleep Solution also addresses common sleep issues such as insomnia, sleep apnea, and restless leg syndrome. The book offers specific yoga poses and techniques that can help alleviate these symptoms and improve the quality of your sleep. By incorporating these practices into your nightly routine, you can create a more restful and rejuvenating sleep experience.

In addition to the physical benefits of restorative yoga, the practice also offers mental and emotional benefits. By focusing on your breath, body, and sensations during your yoga practice, you can cultivate mindfulness and presence, helping to quiet your mind and reduce racing thoughts that can interfere with sleep.

Restorative yoga can also help you cultivate a sense of inner peace and relaxation, allowing you to let go of stress and worries and surrender to the restorative power of sleep.

Overall, The Sleep Solution: Restorative Yoga Practices for Deep Rest is a valuable resource for anyone looking to improve the quality of their sleep. Whether you struggle with insomnia, stress, or simply want to enhance your bedtime routine, this book offers a wealth of information and practical tools to help you create a restful and rejuvenating sleep experience.

By incorporating restorative yoga into your nightly routine, you can create a peaceful and calming environment that promotes deep rest and relaxation. The gentle and therapeutic nature of restorative yoga makes it accessible to people of all ages and fitness levels, making it an ideal practice for anyone looking to improve their sleep quality.

In conclusion, The Sleep Solution: Restorative Yoga Practices for Deep Rest is a comprehensive guide to using restorative yoga to enhance the quality of your sleep.

By incorporating restorative yoga poses, breathing techniques, and mindfulness practices into your bedtime routine, you can create a peaceful and calming environment that promotes deep relaxation and restful sleep.

Whether you struggle with insomnia, stress, or simply want to improve your sleep quality, this book offers a wealth of information and practical tools to help you achieve a more restful and rejuvenating sleep experience.

Restorative Yoga for Better Sleep: A Holistic Approach

Restorative yoga is a gentle form of yoga that focuses on relaxation and stress relief. It involves holding poses for an extended period of time, allowing the body to fully relax and release tension.

This type of yoga is particularly beneficial for those who struggle with sleep issues, as it can help calm the mind and body, promoting a sense of peace and relaxation that can lead to better sleep.

In today's fast-paced world, many people struggle with getting a good night's sleep. Stress, anxiety, and busy schedules can all contribute to sleep disturbances, leaving individuals feeling tired and irritable during the day.

Restorative yoga offers a holistic approach to improving sleep by addressing both the physical and mental aspects of sleep disturbances.

One of the key benefits of restorative yoga for better sleep is its ability to activate the parasympathetic nervous system, also known as the "rest and digest" system. This system is responsible for promoting relaxation and reducing stress, which can help individuals unwind and prepare for sleep.

By practicing restorative yoga before bed, individuals can signal to their bodies that it is time to relax and wind down, making it easier to fall asleep and stay asleep throughout the night.

Restorative yoga also helps release tension in the body, which can be a major obstacle to falling asleep.

Many people carry stress and tension in their muscles, which can lead to discomfort and difficulty relaxing. By holding gentle poses for an extended period of time, restorative yoga allows the muscles to release tension and relax, creating a sense of ease and comfort that can make it easier to drift off to sleep.

In addition to its physical benefits, restorative yoga also has a profound impact on the mind. The practice encourages mindfulness and presence, helping individuals let go of racing thoughts and worries that can keep them awake at night.

By focusing on the breath and the sensations in the body, individuals can cultivate a sense of calm and stillness that can carry over into their sleep, promoting a deeper and more restful night's rest.

To practice restorative yoga for better sleep, it is important to create a calming and comfortable environment. Find a quiet space where you can lay out a yoga mat or blanket, and gather any props you may need, such as bolsters, blankets, or pillows. Dim the lights and create a soothing atmosphere with candles or essential oils toenhance relaxation.

Begin your practice by taking a few moments to center yourself and connect with your breath. Close your eyes and take a few deep breaths, allowing your exhales to be longer than your inhales to activate the parasympatheticnervous system. Set an intention for your practice, such as cultivating peace and calm, and visualize yourself sinking into a state of deep relaxation.

Start your practice with gentle warm-up poses to prepare the body for deeper relaxation. Child's pose, cat-cow, and gentle twists are all great options to help release tension in the spine and hips. Move slowly and mindfully,focusing on the sensations in your body and allowing yourself to let go of any tension or tightness.

Once you feel warmed up, begin to move into restorative poses that support relaxation and rest. Some popular restorative poses for better sleep include supported reclining bound angle pose, supported bridge pose, and legsup the wall pose. Use props to support your body in these poses, allowing yourself to fully relax and release tension.

Hold each pose for several minutes, focusing on your breath and allowing yourself to sink deeper into relaxation with each exhale. If your mind starts to wander, gently bring your focus back to your breath and the sensations in your body. Allow yourself to fully surrender to the pose, letting go of any resistance or tension.

After holding each pose, take a few moments in savasana, or corpse pose, to integrate the benefits of your practice. Allow yourself to fully relax and rest in this final pose, letting go of any remaining tension or stress. Stay in savasana for as long as you need, allowing yourself to fully unwind and prepare for sleep.

As you finish your practice, take a few moments to reflect on how you feel. Notice any changes in your body and mind, and acknowledge the sense of peace and relaxation that you have cultivated. Carry this sense of calm with you as you prepare for bed, allowing yourself to drift off to sleep with ease and grace.

In addition to practicing restorative yoga before bed, there are several other holistic approaches that can support better sleep.

Creating a bedtime routine that includes calming activities, such as reading, taking a warm bath, or practicing meditation, can help signal to your body that it is time to wind down and prepare for sleep.

Avoiding screens and stimulating activities before bed can also promote better sleep by reducing exposure to blue light and stress-inducing stimuli.

Peaceful Night's Sleep

In today's fast-paced world, it can be challenging to find the time to relax and unwind. With the constant demands of work, family, and other responsibilities, many people struggle to get a good night's sleep.

 This lack of rest can have a significant impact on both physical and mental health, leading to increased stress, anxiety, and fatigue. However, there is a solution that can help you find peace and relaxation at the end of a long day: restorative yoga.

Restorative yoga is a gentle and soothing form of yoga that focuses on relaxation and rejuvenation. It involves using props such as blankets, bolsters, and blocks to support the body in various poses, allowing for deep relaxation and release of tension.

Restorative yoga is especially beneficial for those who struggle with insomnia, anxiety, or chronic stress, as it helps to calm the nervous system and promote a sense of inner peace.

In this guide, we will explore the benefits of restorative yoga for sleep, as well as provide you with a step-by-step practice that you can do at home to help you unwind and prepare for a restful night's sleep.

The Benefits of Restorative Yoga for Sleep

Restorative yoga offers a wide range of benefits for both the body and mind, making it an excellent practice for improving sleep quality. Some of the key benefits of restorative yoga for sleep include:

1. Stress Reduction: Restorative yoga helps to calm the nervous system and reduce stress levels, making it easier to relax and fall asleep at night. By focusing on deep breathing and gentle movements, restorative yoga can help you release tension and let go of the worries of the day.

2. Muscle Relaxation: Many people carry tension in their muscles, especially in the neck, shoulders, and back. Restorative yoga poses help to release this tension and promote relaxation in the body, making it easier to unwind and prepare for sleep.

3. Improved Circulation: Restorative yoga poses are designed to open up the body and improve circulation, which can help to promote a sense of relaxation and ease. By allowing blood to flow more freely throughout the body, restorative yoga can help you feel more comfortable and at ease as you prepare for sleep.

4. Mental Clarity: Restorative yoga encourages mindfulness and presence in the moment, helping you to let go of racing thoughts and worries. By focusing on the breath and the body, restorative yoga can help you quiet the mind and find a sense

of inner peace before bedtime.

5. Better Sleep Quality: By promoting relaxation and stress reduction, restorative yoga can help you fall asleep faster and enjoy a deeper, more restful night's sleep. Many people who practice restorative yoga report waking up feeling more refreshed and rejuvenated, ready to face the day ahead.

A Step-by-Step Restorative Yoga Practice for Sleep

Now that you understand the benefits of restorative yoga for sleep, let's explore a simple and soothing practice that you can do at home to help you unwind and prepare for a peaceful night's sleep. You will need a few props

for this practice, including a yoga mat, a bolster or a few firm pillows, a blanket, and a yoga block or two.

1. Supported Child's Pose (Balasana)

Begin your practice by coming into a supported child's pose. Place a bolster or a few pillows lengthwise on your mat, then kneel down and lower your torso onto the props. Rest your forehead on the bolster or pillows and extend your arms out in front of you, palms facing down. Take a few deep breaths here, allowing your body to relax and release tension.

2. Supported Bridge Pose (Setu Bandhasana)

Next, come into a supported bridge pose to open up the chest and shoulders. Lie on your back with your knees bent and feet hip-width apart.

Place a block or a bolster under your sacrum and lower back, then allow your armsto rest by your sides with palms facing up. Close your eyes and breathe deeply, feeling the chest and shoulders open up with each inhale.

3. Supported Legs-Up-The-Wall Pose (Viparita Karani)

Move into a supported legs-up-the-wall pose to promote circulation and relaxation in the legs. Sit sideways nextto a wall with your knees bent, then swing your legs up the wall as you lie down on your back.

Place a blanket under your hips for support, then relax your arms by your sides with palms facing up. Close your eyes and breathe deeply, feeling the tension release from your legs and lower back.

4. Supported Reclining Twist (Supta Matsyendrasana)

Finish your practice with a supported reclining twist to release tension in the spine and promote relaxation. Lie on your back with your knees bent and feet hip-width apart, then extend your arms out to the sides in a T shape.

Chapter 12: Sleep Better with Restorative Yoga: A Comprehensive Guide to Relaxation

In today's fast-paced world, getting a good night's sleep can sometimes feel like an impossible task. Between work stress, family responsibilities, and the constant bombardment of technology, it's no wonder that so many people struggle with sleep issues.

However, there is a natural and effective solution that can help you get the restyou need – restorative yoga.

Restorative yoga is a gentle and relaxing form of yoga that focuses on deep relaxation and stress relief. By incorporating restorative yoga into your daily routine, you can improve your sleep quality, reduce anxiety and stress, and promote overall well-being.

In this comprehensive guide, we will explore the benefits of restorative yoga for sleep, as well as provide you with a variety of poses and techniques to help you get the rest you deserve.

The Connection Between Yoga and Sleep

Yoga has been practiced for thousands of years and is known

for its numerous health benefits, including improved flexibility, strength, and mental clarity. However, many people are unaware of the powerful connection between yoga and sleep. By incorporating yoga into your daily routine, you can improve your sleepquality in a number of ways.

One of the main reasons why yoga is so effective for sleep is because it helps to calm the mind and relax the body. Many people struggle to fall asleep at night because their minds are racing with thoughts and worries. By practicing yoga, you can quiet the mind and release tension in the body, making it easier to drift off to sleep.

Additionally, yoga helps to regulate the nervous system, which can have a positive impact on your sleep patterns. When the nervous system is in a state of balance, it can help to reduce stress and anxiety, two common culprits of sleep disturbances.

By practicing yoga regularly, you can train your body to relax and unwind, making it easier to fall asleep and stay asleep throughout the night.

The Benefits of Restorative Yoga for Sleep

Restorative yoga is a specific style of yoga that focuses on relaxation and rejuvenation. Unlike more active forms of yoga, such as vinyasa or power yoga, restorative yoga involves holding gentle poses for an extended period of time, often with the support of props like blankets, bolsters, and pillows. This allows the body to fully relax and release tension, promoting deep rest and restoration.

There are many benefits of restorative yoga for sleep, including:

1. Stress Reduction: Restorative yoga helps to activate the parasympathetic nervous system, also known as the "rest and digest" system. This can help to lower cortisol levels and reduce stress, making it easier to relax and fallasleep.

2. Improved Circulation: Many restorative yoga poses are designed to improve circulation and blood flow, which can help to promote relaxation and prepare the body for sleep.

3. Muscle Relaxation: By holding gentle poses for an extended period of time, restorative yoga can help to release tension in the muscles and promote deep relaxation.

4. Mindfulness: Restorative yoga encourages mindfulness and present-moment awareness, which can help to quiet the mind and reduce racing thoughts that can interfere with sleep.

5. Better Breathing: Restorative yoga often incorporates deep breathing techniques, which can help to calm the nervous system and promote relaxation.

Overall, restorative yoga is a powerful tool for improving sleep quality and promoting overall well-being. By incorporating restorative yoga into your daily routine, you can experience the many benefits of deep relaxationand rejuvenation.

Restorative Yoga Poses for Better Sleep

There are a variety of restorative yoga poses that can help to promote relaxation and improve sleep quality. Hereare some of the best poses to try before bedtime:

1. Supported Child's Pose: This pose is a gentle forward bend that helps to release tension in the back and shoulders. To practice this pose, place a bolster or pillow lengthwise on your mat and kneel in front of it.

2. Loweryour chest onto the bolster and extend your arms out in front of you. Rest your forehead on the mat and breathe deeply, allowing your body to relax and unwind.

3. Legs-Up-the-Wall Pose: This pose is a gentle inversion that can help to calm the nervous system and promote relaxation. To practice this pose, lie on your back with your hips close to a wall.

Extend your legs up the wall andrelax your arms by your sides. Close your eyes and focus on your breath, allowing your body to release tension and stress.

4. Supported Bridge Pose: This pose helps to open the chest

and release tension in the back and shoulders.

To practice this pose, lie on your back with your knees bent and feet hip-width apart. Place a block or bolster underyour sacrum and lift your hips towards the ceiling. Rest your arms by your sides and breathe deeply, allowing your body to relax and unwind.

Conclusion

In the serene sanctuary of restorative yoga, you've embarked on a transformative journey, one that promises to banish the shackles of insomnia and welcome the embrace of rejuvenating sleep. Throughout this sacred exploration, you've discovered the power of relaxation, the potency of presence, and the magic of mindful movement.

As you conclude this enchanting odyssey, remember this: serenity is not merely a destination but a path we tread each night as we surrender to the gentle whispers of tranquility. With each pose, each breath, and each moment of stillness, you've unraveled the knots of tension, paving the way for a night of deep, restorative rest.

So, my fellow traveler on the road to blissful nights, let us carry forth the wisdom gleaned from these pages. Let us embrace the practice of restorative yoga as a sacred ritual, a sanctuary where we nurture our bodies, soothe our souls, and reclaim our birthright to sleep like royalty.

With each nightfall, may you find solace in the arms of serenity, and may your dreams be woven with threads of tranquility. Remember, dear reader, the power to unlock serenity and banish insomnia lies within you. Embrace it, cherish it, and let it guide you on your journey to blissful nights and rejuvenated days.

Rest deeply, dream sweetly, and awaken refreshed, for you are the architect of your own tranquility. Until we meet again under the stars of serenity, may your path be illuminated by the light of peaceful slumber.

Biography

Meet Helenna Lemann, a radiant soul dedicated to guiding others on their journey to wellness and tranquility. As the author of the captivating book, "Soothe Your Soul, Sleep Like Royalty: Unveil the Sacred Art of Restorative Yoga for Blissful Nights," Helenna brings a wealth of knowledge and a passion for holistic living to her readers.

With a background rooted in the ancient practice of yoga, Helenna's expertise shines brightly as she shares her insights into the transformative power of restorative yoga. Her gentle yet profound understanding of the body, mind, and spirit allows her to craft expertly curated poses and yoga scripts designed to melt away tension and invite deep, restorative rest.

Beyond her dedication to yoga and wellness, Helenna is also an avid explorer of the inner realms of relaxation and mindfulness. When she's not writing or teaching yoga, you can often find her immersed in the world of holistic healing, exploring new ways to promote harmony and balance in her own life and the lives of others.

Helenna's boundless enthusiasm for her work is infectious, inspiring readers to embark on their own journey toward inner peace and rejuvenation. With her ebook as your guide, you'll discover the transformative power of restorative yoga and unlock the secrets to blissful nights and revitalized days. So, join Helenna on this enchanting odyssey and prepare to awaken to a life filled with serenity, joy, and boundless possibilities.

www.ingramcontent.com/pod-product-compliance
Lightning Source LLC
Chambersburg PA
CBHW071007250726
48653CB00005B/1552